ESSENTIAL DK COMPUTERS

WINDOWS Me
MILLENNIUM EDITION

About This Book

Windows Me: Millennium Edition is intended for those who are new to computers and who need an introductory guide to Microsoft's recently introduced PC operating system.

Beginning to use a computer for the first time is inevitably difficult. There is no other gadget that you can compare a computer to, nor one that can have provided you with any experience to draw on. This is where our book can help. We show you what the different elements of the opening screen mean once you've turned your computer on, and we advise you on how to use the mouse. The two basic elements of windows and their menus are covered, which naturally lead into how to start using a few of the programs that are provided with Windows Me. Using these programs creates collections of your work, called files, and we tell you how to manage them. Installing software is considered, as is connecting to the internet. Finally, for your relaxation, we show you how to play games on your PC.

The chapters and the subsections present the information using step-by-step

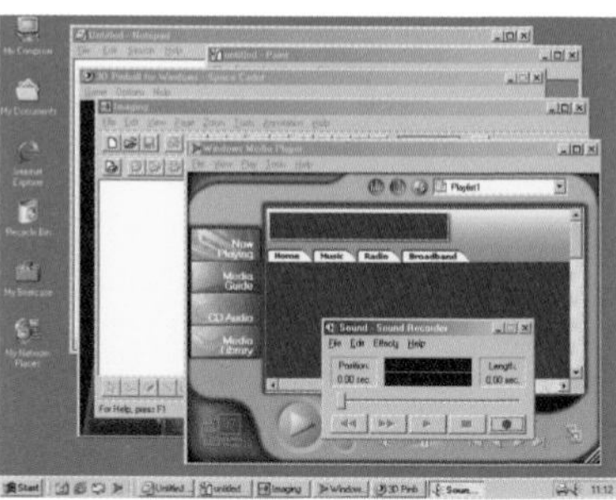

sequences. Virtually every step is accompanied by an illustration showing how your screen should look at each stage.

The book contains several features to help you understand both what is happening and what you need to do.

Command keys, such as ENTER and CTRL, are shown in these rectangles: Enter and Ctrl, so that there's no confusion, for example, over whether you should press that key or type the letters "ctrl."

Cross-references are shown in the text as left- or right-hand page icons: and . The page number and the reference are shown at the foot of the page.

As well as the step-by-step sections, there are boxes that explain a feature in detail, and tip boxes that provide alternative methods. Finally, at the back, you will find a glossary of common terms and a comprehensive index.

WINDOWS Me MILLENNIUM EDITION

ANDREW EASTON

LONDON, NEW YORK, SYDNEY, DELHI,
PARIS, MUNICH, and JOHANNESBURG

Senior Editor Amy Corzine
Senior Art Editor Sarah Cowley
DTP Designer Julian Dams
Production Controller Michelle Thomas

Managing Editor Adèle Hayward
Senior Managing Art Editor Nigel Duffield

Produced for Dorling Kindersley Limited by
Design Revolution Limited, Queens Park Villa,
30 West Drive, Brighton, East Sussex BN2 2GE
Editorial Director Ian Whitelaw
Senior Designer Andy Ashdown
Project Editor John Watson
Designer Andrew Easton

First published in Great Britain in 2001 by
Dorling Kindersley Limited,
9 Henrietta Street, London WC2E 8PS

2 4 6 8 10 9 7 5 3 1

A CIP catalogue record for this book is available from the British Library.

ISBN 0-7513-3360-3

Colour reproduced by Colourscan, Singapore
Printed and bound in Italy by Graphicom

For our complete catalogue visit
www.dk.com

Contents

WINDOWS ME

Windows Me has been developed with the home PC user in mind, and with this latest offering, Microsoft is aiming to make the PC an even better environment in which to work.

WHAT IS WINDOWS ME?

Windows Me is an operating system – the backbone of your day-to-day computing environment. Windows Me has simplified the PC experience by removing some irritations of earlier versions of Windows and introducing improvements of its own.

RECOGNIZE ME?

In the early 1990s, Microsoft released its first version of Windows, known as Windows 3.x (the "x" stood for the different version numbers). This was a great leap forward from the old operating system, known as MS-DOS. In 1995, Windows 95 was released, which was a smaller step forward than 3.x. Three years later, Windows 98 appeared, and was an even smaller step forward than the 95 version. The release of Windows Millennium Edition (Me) is an even smaller advance, but it's still an improvement on its immediate predecessor.

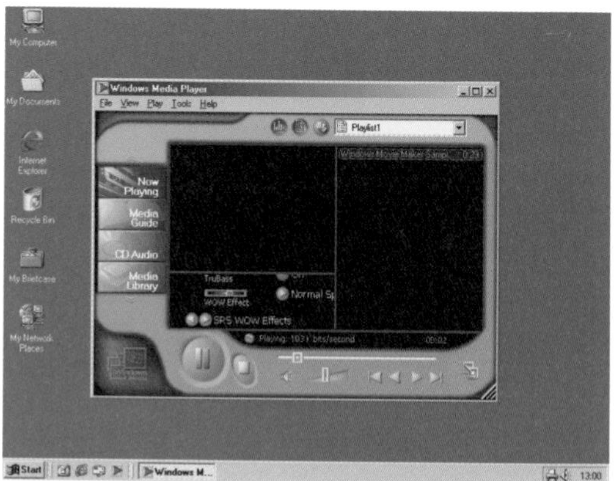

Technically Speaking...
Windows is a Graphical User Interface (GUI), which means that instead of typing commands into your computer as MS-DOS required, you use a mouse to point and click to issue instructions to the machine.

FEATURES OF WINDOWS ME FOR EXPERIENCED USERS

• MEDIA PLAYER

Media Player can access digital media on the internet, from movies to radio stations. You can also download and play MP3 files. A database called Media Library lets you organize MP3 files, audio, WAVs, and video files into one source. You can also copy CDs to your hard disk in Windows Media Audio format.

• MOVIE MAKER

Movie Maker captures video off a camcorder, VCR, or webcam and lets you edit the footage before saving it as a movie. Connect your camera to your PC then click on the record button. Movie Maker imports your video and automatically breaks it into compressed clips for easier management and manipulation. Digital photos for slide shows can be imported, and background music and narration can be added. You are likely to need additional hardware, such as a video capture card to transfer the video from your camcorder or VCR.

• HOME NETWORKING

Windows Me features Universal Plug and Play, which enables devices to be connected and to share resources. Connecting PCs used to be complicated, but with the Windows Me Home Networking Wizard, creating a home network is easy. It is also possible to connect digital music players, digital cameras and camcorders, and wireless devices over a network. For example, a clock radio and a thermostat could communicate over the network to turn on the heating before the alarm goes off in the morning.

• AUTOUPDATE

AutoUpdate allows the latest enhancements to Windows Me to be downloaded automatically. When you are online, AutoUpdate uses the occasions when the modem is inactive to download updates. When an update is fully downloaded, AutoUpdate informs you and provides an opportunity to install the update. AutoUpdate is easily configurable and provides a convenient way to keep your computer system current.

• SYSTEM FILE PROTECTION

System File Protection (SFP) prevents problems before they occur by stopping the accidental or unauthorized overwriting of system files and helps keep the system stable. For example, a new application may try to overwrite a system file with an older or an altered file, which can affect the system's stability. SFP does not allow any correct system files to be overwritten.

• SYSTEM RESTORE

The System Restore feature enables the computer's system to be returned easily to its previous settings. For example, if a newly installed application is causing problems, the computer can be returned to its preinstallation settings. Users can choose a date as a restore point, such as the point before the new installation, or one of the predefined system checkpoints.

THE WINDOWS ME DESKTOP

When you first start your computer, the Windows Me desktop appears. It is from this location that every action that you carry out on your computer begins. From here, you can launch programs, search for documents, surf the internet, and play games. The desktop is also a place where you can keep all your letters, documents, photographs, and much more. The desktop is also highly customizable.

FEATURES KEY

❶ My Computer
The My Computer window displays all the folders, documents, and programs on your computer.

❷ My Documents
The My Documents folder is a place to store any files you need. For example, you may create other folders within it, separating your graphics files from your text documents.

❸ Internet Explorer
If your computer is set up correctly, then double-clicking this icon [page icon] *will connect you to the internet.*

❹ Recycle Bin
The Recycle Bin [page icon] *is where you place items that you want to delete.*

❺ My Briefcase
My Briefcase allows you to carry work between two computers, and makes sure that the files are up-to-date on both hard disk drives.

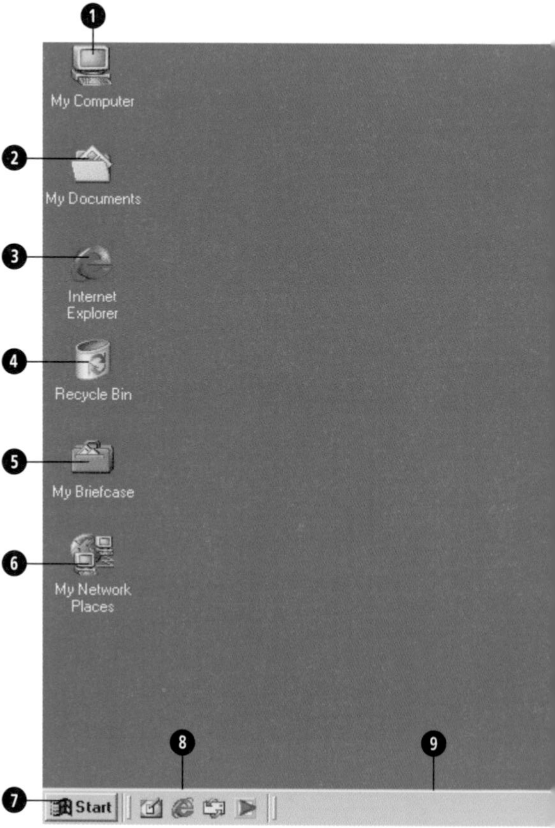

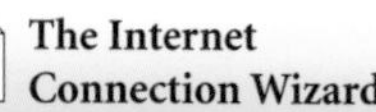
49 **The Internet Connection Wizard**

41 **Deleting Unwanted Files**

STARTUP PROBLEMS?

When you turn on your PC, it should go through a procedure known as booting up. If this fails to happen, or if the computer fails to start up as it should, carry out these checks. First make sure that the power cable is plugged in and that the power is turned on. Second, check there isn't a floppy disk in the floppy disk drive. Third, check all interconnecting cabling from the PC.

FEATURES KEY

6 My Network Places
This tool links your computer to any others that are on the same network.

7 Start Button
The Start button provides a tree structure of shortcuts to the document folders, files, and programs stored on the computer.

8 The Quick Launch Toolbar
Add or remove applications to access them easily.

9 Taskbar
The Taskbar gives quick access to programs and documents that are open on your desktop.

10 System Tray
The System Tray contains the icons of special utilities.

11 The Desktop
The Windows Me desktop is where you work. Programs open here, and you can store files for as long as you need.

WELCOME TO ME

Now that we have seen the Windows Me desktop, it's time to explore your surroundings further and discover what the taskbar does, as well as the different menus and help screens.

USING THE TASKBAR

The taskbar is a panel initially located at the foot of the screen. It contains the Start button, from where programs can be launched, the Quick Launch bar, the System tray, and the buttons for all your open files, programs, and windows.

NAVIGATING BETWEEN WINDOWS

● As you use, experiment, and play with Windows Me, you will find that you can easily have many different applications and windows open at the same time, and that your screen may resemble the example on the right.

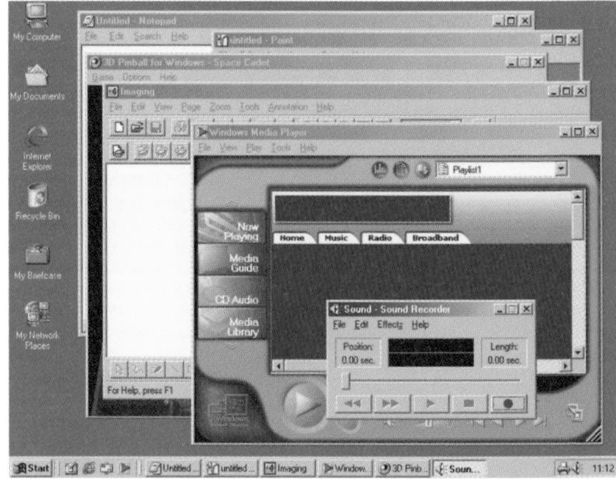

All the documents and windows that are active have a corresponding button on the taskbar

● Clicking on a program button on the taskbar brings the program to the foreground where it is ready to use. Here, we have clicked on the **3D Pinball for Windows** button to open its window.

Note that 3D Pinball for Windows is now in the foreground and active

Clicking on a button makes the application active

USING THE MOUSE BUTTONS

Generally speaking, the left mouse button is used to activate applications or menu options by clicking once. It is also used for scrolling through windows and menus, and for dragging and dropping. If you right-click with the mouse on an object, for instance, the **My Computer** icon on the desktop, a menu of options appears (right). This allows you, among other options, to open, browse, create a shortcut to, rename, and view the properties of that object.

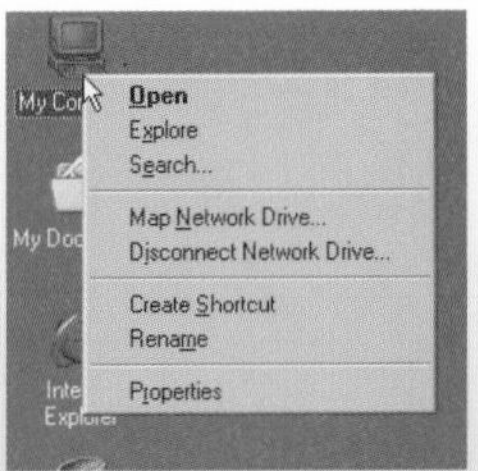

13 **Using the Start Menu**

37 **Moving a File Between Locations**

MINIMIZING ALL WINDOWS

- To minimize all windows when you start to lose track of where they all are, right-click on a blank area of the taskbar and click on **Minimize All Windows.**

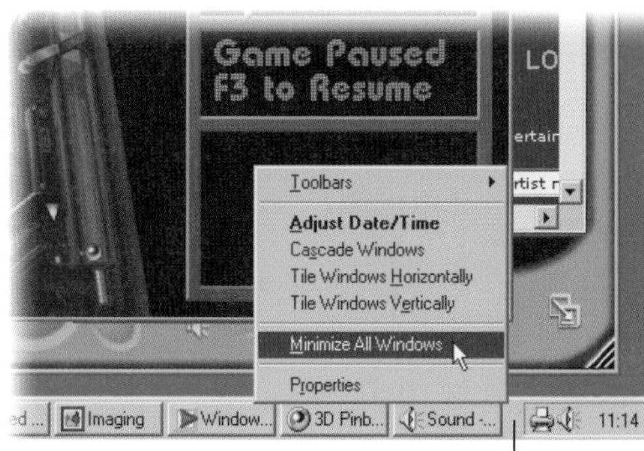

Right click in a blank space

RESTORING A WINDOW

- All the applications have been minimized and the desktop is clear. However, any one of the windows can still be accessed through the taskbar by left-clicking on its taskbar button.

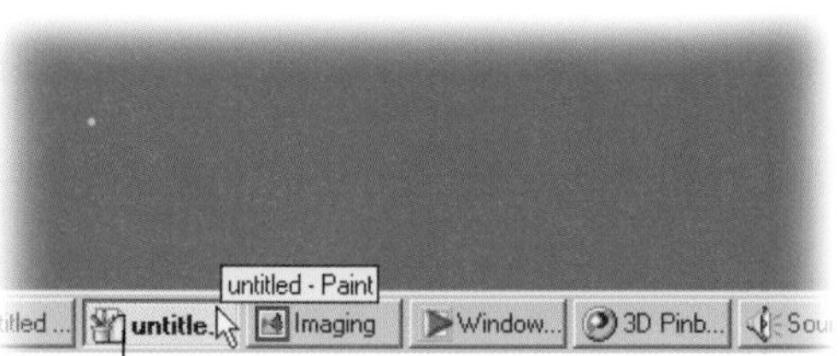

Single-click on the application that you wish to use; in this case we have clicked on ***Paint*** *and the application opens*

MINIMIZING AND MAXIMIZING INDIVIDUAL WINDOWS

❶ Minimize
Clicking on this button minimizes the window. The window is still available by left-clicking on its button on the taskbar.

❷ Maximize
The Maximize button expands the window to fill the whole screen. Once maximized, the button then changes its name to ***Restore.***

❸ Restore
Clicking on the ***Restore*** *button returns the window to its previous dimensions and location onscreen.*

❹ Close
To shut down an application or to close a window, such as Windows Explorer, click the ***Close*** *button. If you need to save an open file before closing, Windows prompts you.*

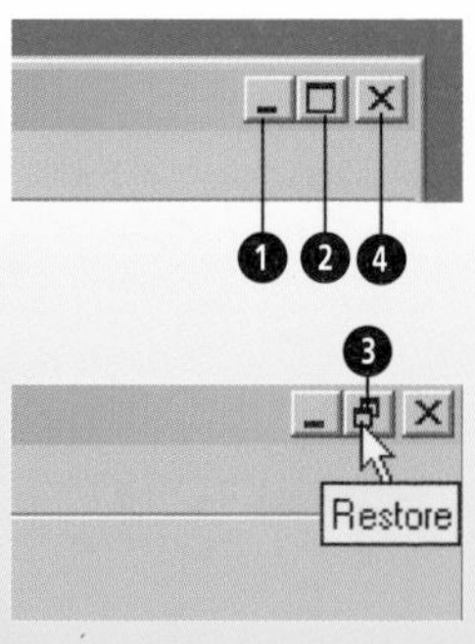

USING THE START MENU

The Windows **Start** button is the main starting point for finding and accessing files and documents, installing and using programs, and changing and customizing the settings on your computer to suit your own requirements. It is also the location from where you can access the **Help** options, and, paradoxically, is the place where can you restart your computer or shut it down at the end of a session.

OPENING THE START MENU

- Place the cursor over the **Start** button and click the left mouse button once.
- The Start menu pops up. Any of the options can be clicked on to select it. When the options that are accompanied by a black, right-pointing arrowhead are clicked on, they display a submenu of further options.

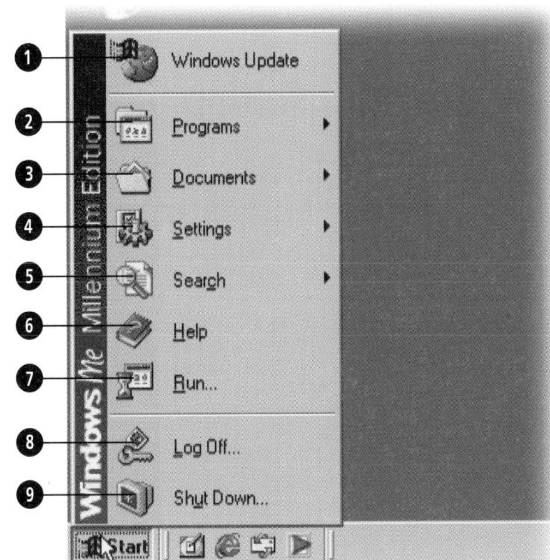

START MENU KEY

1. Windows Update *see* p.7
2. Programs Menu *see* p.14
3. Documents Menu *see* p.19
4. Settings Menu *see* p.16
5. Search Menu *see* p.17
6. Windows Help *see* p.52
7. Run Command *see* p.15
8. Log Off Option *To log off as a user*
9. Shut Down Option *see* p.19.

THE PROGRAMS MENU

The **Programs** menu lists the software, sometimes called "applications," that you use to perform tasks on your computer.

The **Programs** submenu also allows access to further submenus where related applications are grouped together.

PROGRAMS SUBMENU

- When you initially move the cursor over the **Programs** entry in the **Start** menu, the submenu may contain one or two entries.
- The rest of the menu can be seen by clicking on the two down arrowheads.

Windows Me "tidies" items that haven't been used recently by placing them in a subordinate part of the menu

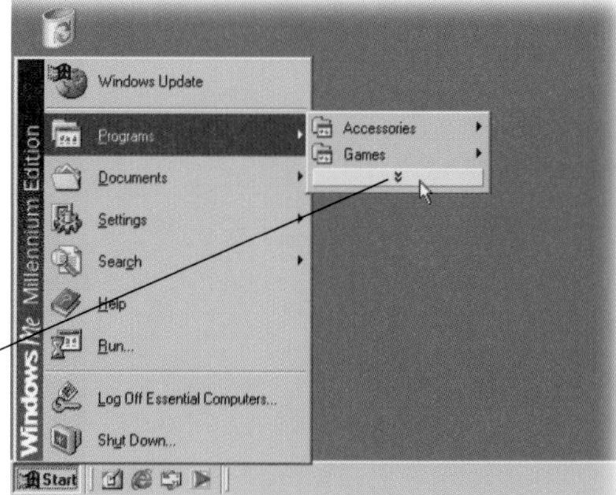

- When the down arrowheads are clicked, they display these hidden, less used, applications.

*The **Online Services** submenu contains connections to the internet*

*Clicking on this option immediately launches **Windows Media Player***

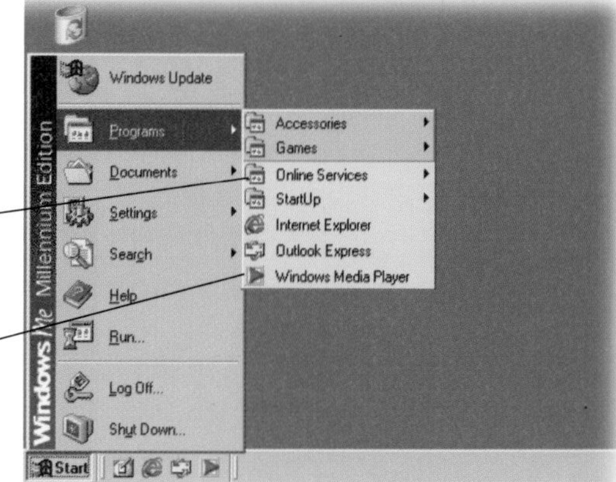

ACCESSORIES

● The Accessories menu contains applications that are installed along with Windows Me. They include games, a calculator, and text-editing tools.

● In addition, this menu also contains its own submenus.

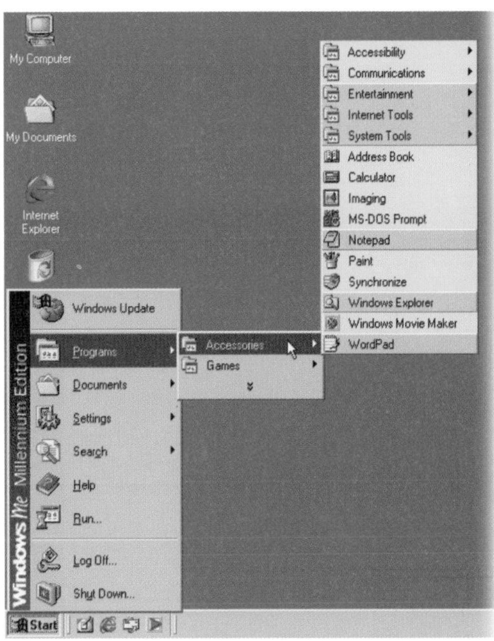

The Run Command

An alternative method of launching a program is to click on **Run** in the **Start** menu and type the name of the file that is needed to run the program. This option is generally used by more experienced users of Microsoft Windows.

GAMES

● The **Games** submenu contains a selection of simple applications for passing time.

● Not only are there a number of games that can be played on your own, but there are also five that can be played over the internet. With Windows Me, you can now play games from your office against someone sitting on the other side of the world.

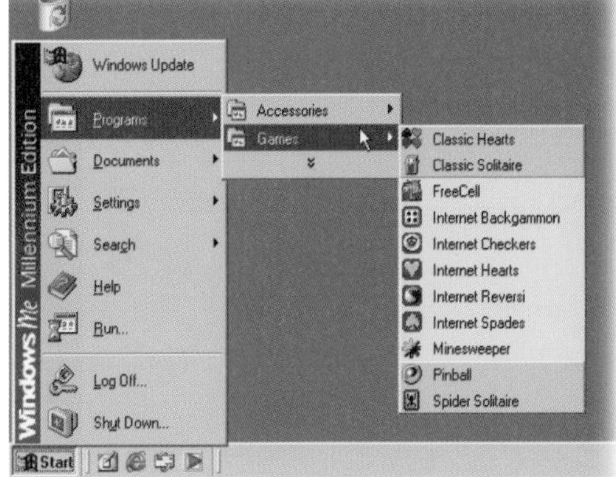

THE SETTINGS MENU

The **Settings** menu contains options that include the opportunity to customize and fine-tune the working of your computer, to connect to another computer, to handle printers, and to select what appears in the taskbar and the **Start** menu.

SETTINGS

● The **Settings** menu has four main options: The **Control Panel**, **Dial-Up Networking**, the **Printers** folder, and **Taskbar and Start Menu.**

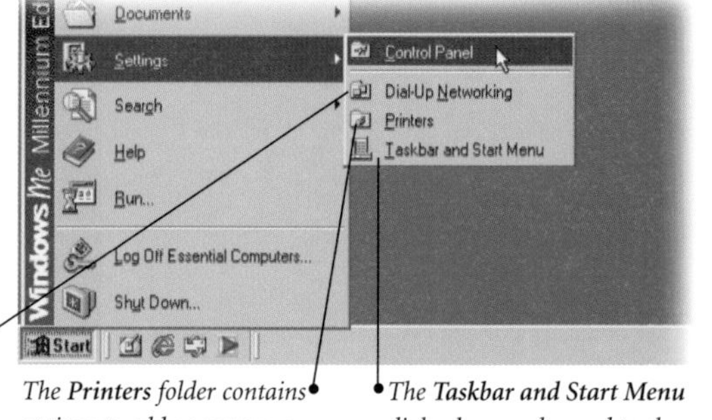

Dial-Up Networking enables you to connect to another computer and to a network by using a modem

*The **Printers** folder contains options to add or remove a printer from your computer*

*The **Taskbar and Start Menu** dialog box can be used to change the way that items are viewed*

THE CONTROL PANEL OPTIONS

● The **Control Panel** has options available to alter many of the settings on your computer. It also has facilities to add and remove hardware and programs, alter the settings for your peripherals and network, and it also includes **Accessibility Options.**

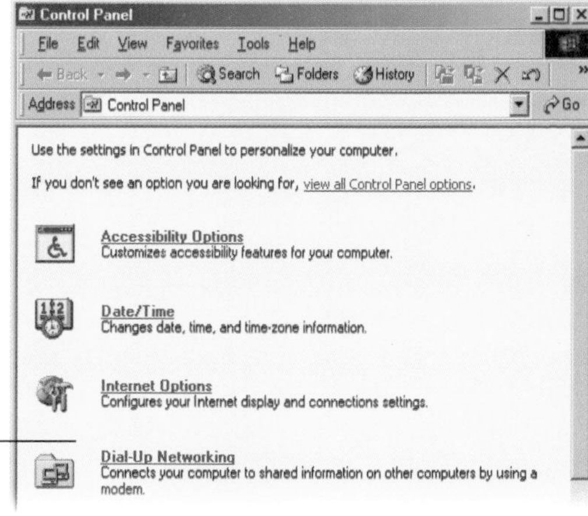

*The **Control Panel** contains many options for customizing your PC*

THE SEARCH MENU

The Search menu has three options. The first is to search for files and folders contained on your computer, the second and third options allow you to search for websites and for people – for these latter two options, internet access is needed 📄.

1 SELECTING FILES OR FOLDERS

● Click once on the **Start** button, select **Search**, move the cursor across to **For Files or Folders** in the submenu, and click once.

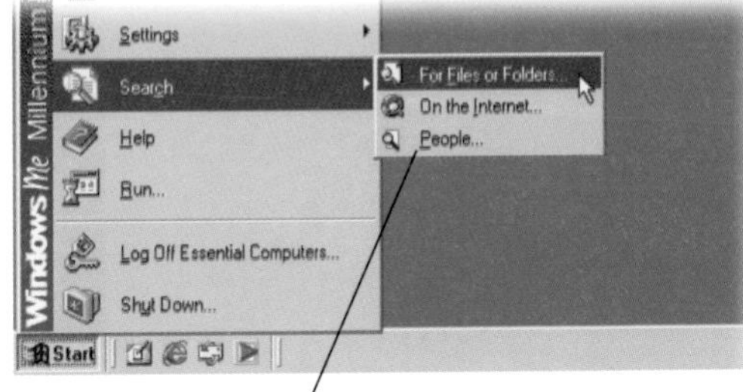

There are also the options to search ***On the Internet*** *and for* ***People****; you will need your computer to be connected to the internet to use these options*

2 ENTERING THE SEARCH DETAILS

● The **Search Results** dialog box opens. Click inside the text box below **Search for files or folders named.** Enter as much of the name as you can. In this example, a missing **Letter** is being searched for.

● The next box down, labeled **Containing text,** allows you to enter words contained in the file. The letter we are looking for here has the date **May**, so this is entered into the box.

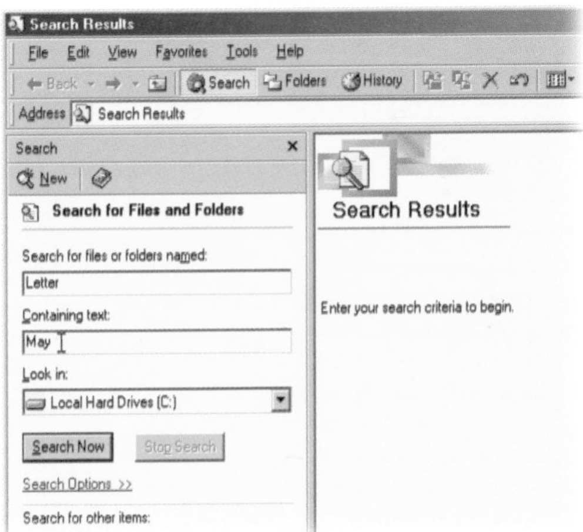

3 NARROWING THE SEARCH

- To tell the computer where specifically to search for the file, click on the arrow next to the text box labeled **Look in**. In this instance, the file should be contained in the folder **My Documents**. In the list, click on **My Documents** so that it appears in the box.
- Click on **Search Now**.

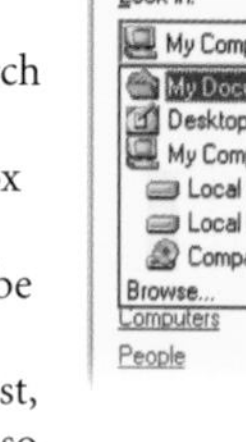

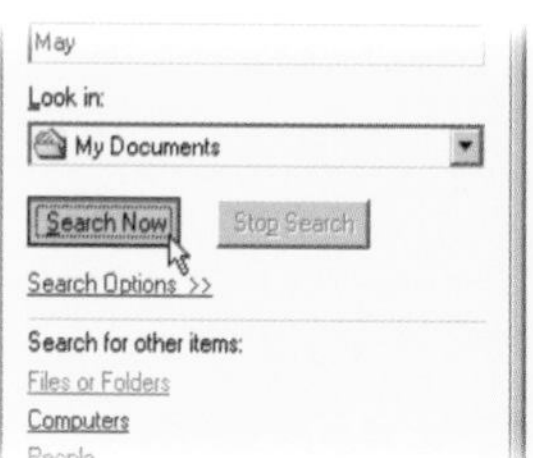

4 VIEWING THE RESULTS

- Any files that match your search criteria are shown in the right-hand panel.
- Once you have found the file, you will be able to see its exact location by clicking on it once. At the top of the window, the location is now displayed as a hyperlink, which means that you can click on it to go straight to the folder in which the file is contained.
- If you want to open the file immediately, you can do so by simply double-clicking on it.

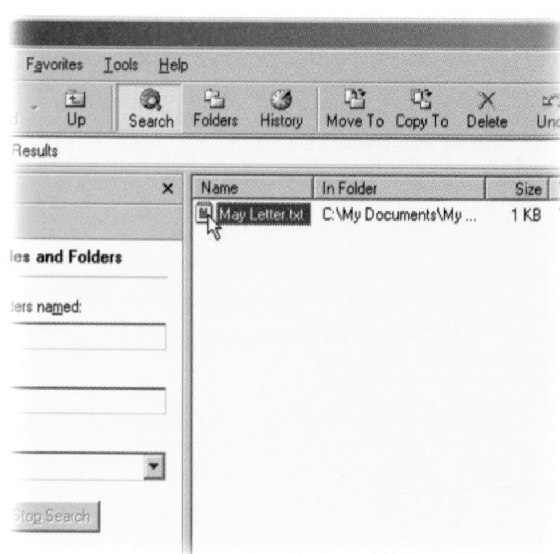

THE DOCUMENTS OPTION

• The **Documents** option on the Start menu opens documents that you have been working on recently. Click on the **Start** menu, point to **Documents,** move the cursor over the document that you want to open, and click on it.

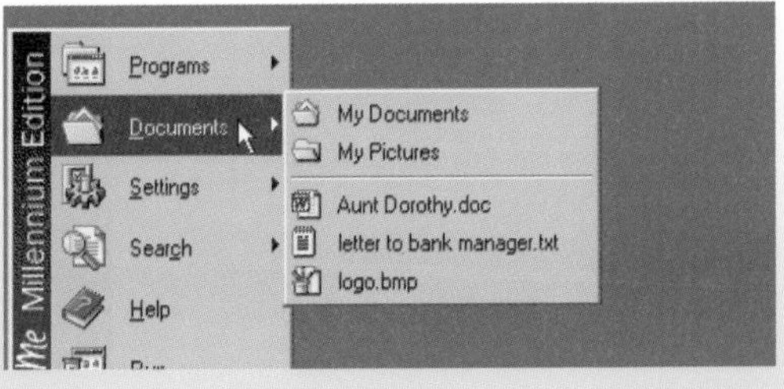

RESTARTING AND SHUTTING DOWN

Turning off a computer is different from switching off the television. There are internal settings that a computer has to maintain, and these have to be recorded before shutdown. However, with Windows Me, shutting down is now much faster.

1 LAUNCHING SHUT DOWN

• Click on the **Start** button and click on **Shut Down.**

2 SELECTING THE RIGHT OPTION

• **Shut down** is the first option on the menu.
• **Restart** is the equivalent of shutting down and starting again.
• **Stand by** puts your computer into a low power-consumption mode.
• When the correct selection is highlighted, click on **OK.**

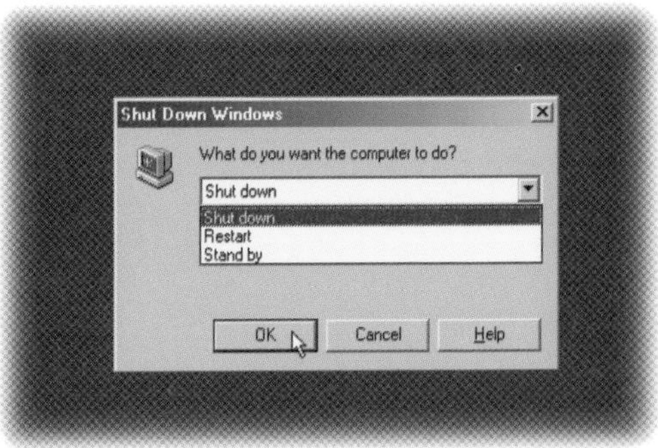

WINDOWS ME PROGRAMS

When you start Windows Me, and a take a look around for the first time, you will notice that there are various programs available for use. Let's take a look at a few of them.

NOTEPAD

Notepad is a basic text editor, used mainly for creating, viewing, and editing documents that only contain text, and do not contain any images.

Notepad has some very useful features. Text can be cut, copied, and pasted; and there is also an option to add the date and time if you want to include those details.

1 LAUNCHING NOTEPAD

- The first step in using any program or tool on a computer is to open or "launch" it. There may be "shortcuts" available, but to begin with, using the **Start** button is the simplest method.
- Click on the **Start** button, move to **Programs**, **Accessories**, and then finally to **Notepad**.

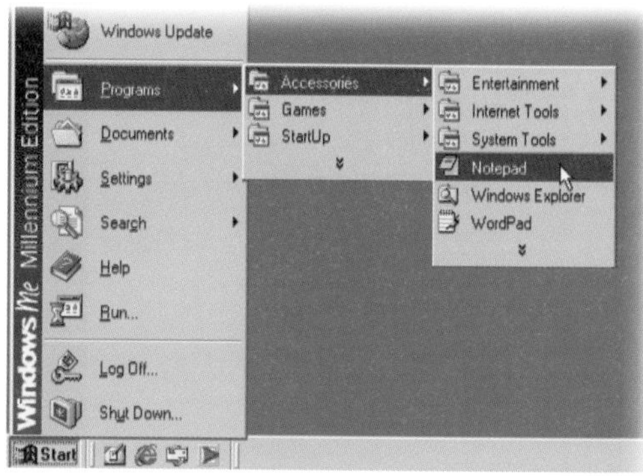

WHAT IS A PROGRAM?

A program allows you to perform a specific task or function on your computer. Programs can also be called "applications," which is a slightly broader term. Programs and applications are also called software. Windows Me is a piece of software that creates a "platform" for other applications.

2 THE NEW DOCUMENT

● A new, blank document screen opens with a blue title bar at the top and a menu bar below it.
● A cursor flashes at the top left of the window and shows where text will appear when you begin typing.

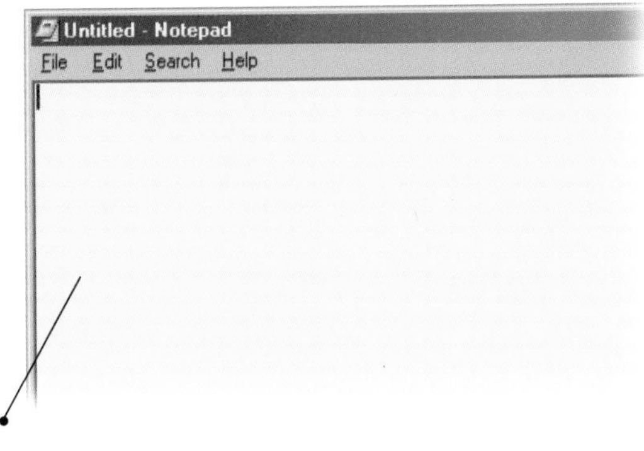

*The **Notepad** main window*

● When you begin typing, the cursor disappears.

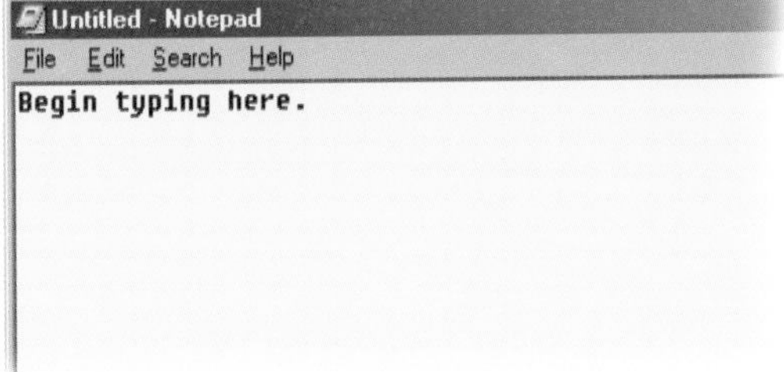

3 SAVING THE DOCUMENT

● Once you have created your first document, you can save it. This allows it to be opened again at any time.
● When you save a file for the first time, Windows asks you to give it a name and select a location where it is to be saved on your hard drive.
● Click on **File** in the Menu bar, and from the drop-down menu click on **Save**.

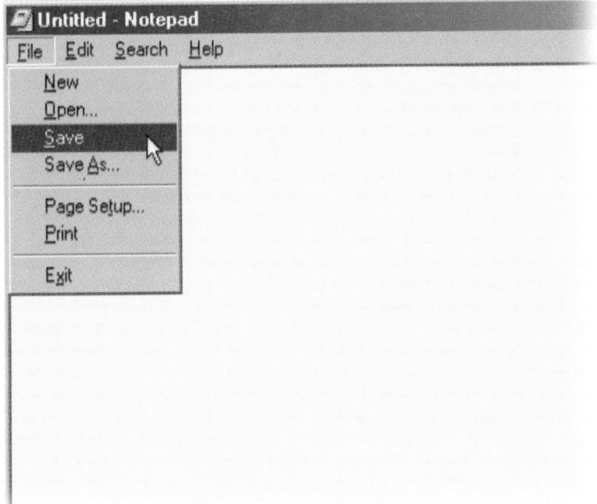

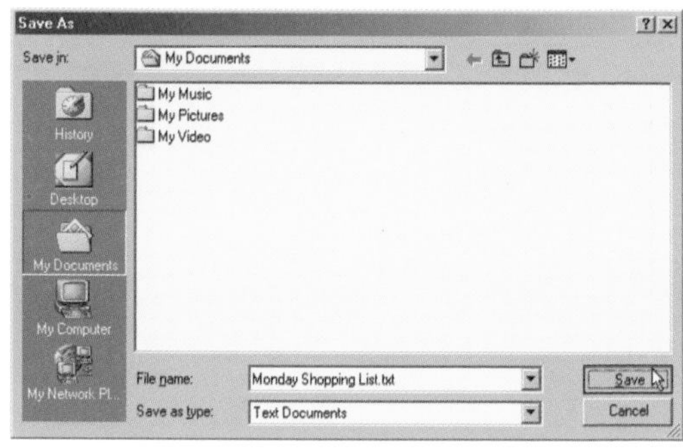

● The **Save As** dialog box opens. By default, Windows directs the file to the **My Documents** folder, which is a useful location for your files when you first start.

● In the **File name** text box, type in a descriptive name for the document.

● Click on the **Save** button. The **Save As** box closes and your document is saved.

4 OPENING AN EXISTING FILE

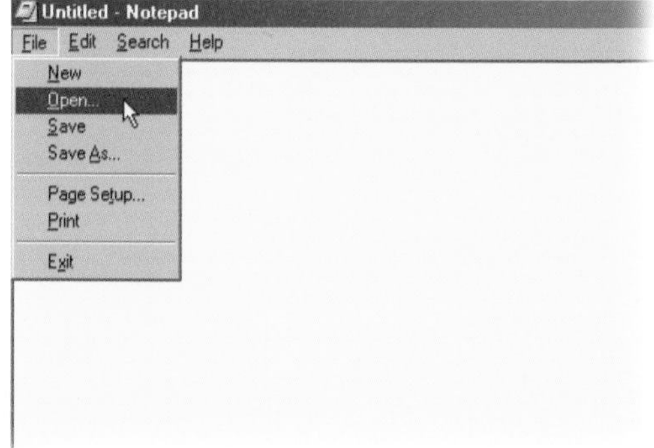

● At some time, you are likely to need to open a file that you have saved to edit it or print it out. There are two main ways of opening a file.

● The first method is carried out from inside Notepad. Open Notepad as before, then click on **File** in the Menu bar, and click on **Open**.

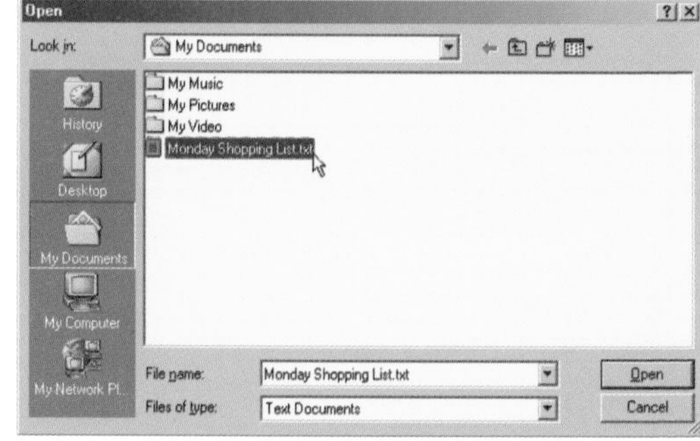

● The **Open** dialog box opens. Notepad makes the assumption, by default, that any documents created previously have been saved to the **My Documents** folder.

● Click on the file that you wish to open (in this case, the **Monday Shopping List.txt**).

- Now move the cursor down to the **Open** button at the bottom right hand corner and click on it.
- The file will open onscreen and you can make changes and then resave it.

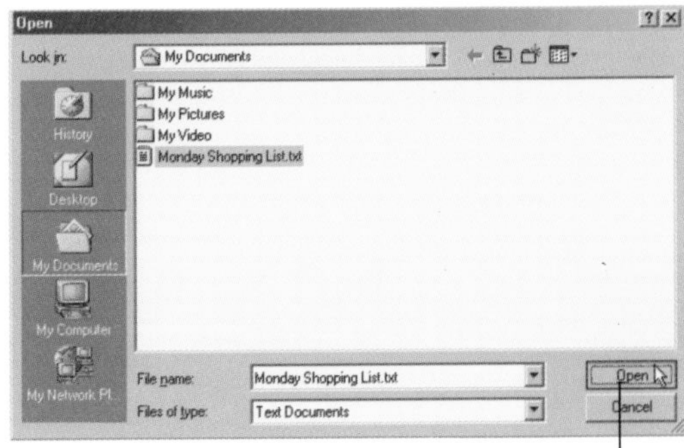

*Click on the **Open** button*

- The second method of opening an existing file is more direct than the first.
- Select the folder that contains the file you want to open. In this case, it is the **My Documents** folder. Double-click on the folder icon to open its window.
- In the **My Documents** window, double-click on the file that you wish to open. The file automatically opens in the program that was used to create it – in this case, Notepad.

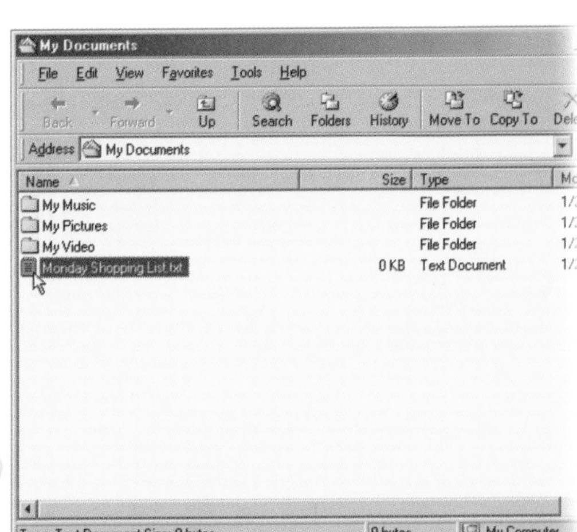

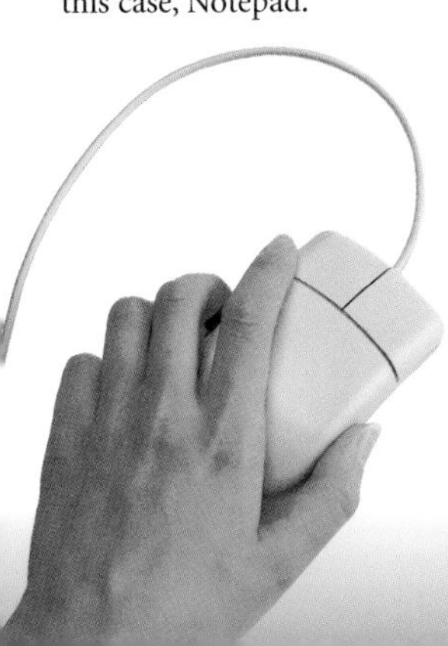

PAINT

Paint is a piece of graphics software that is used to create and work with images. An image you have created can then be pasted into another document, and you can even edit photographs that have been scanned in. Paint also has its own text tool.

LAUNCHING PAINT

- You can launch Paint in the same way that Notepad was launched. Click on the **Start** button, move up to **Programs**, select **Accessories** from the submenu, and then click on **Paint**.
- A window opens that contains painting tools, a color palette, and the main Paint window.

The main Paint window

DRAWING WITH PAINT

- Using the **Pencil** tool, we have drawn an outline of a tree, and then with the **Airbrush** tool we have started to color the image.

*The **Pencil** tool*

*The **Color palette** from which you can select a color by clicking on it*

20 Launching Notepad

THE FINISHED DRAWING

● Using various shades of colors from the color palette, we have created a reasonable representation of a tree. Further efforts will improve with practice.

THE PAINT TOOLS PALETTE

● There are many tools available in Paint, from a simple line tool to an airbrush. With time and patience, these tools can soon be mastered.

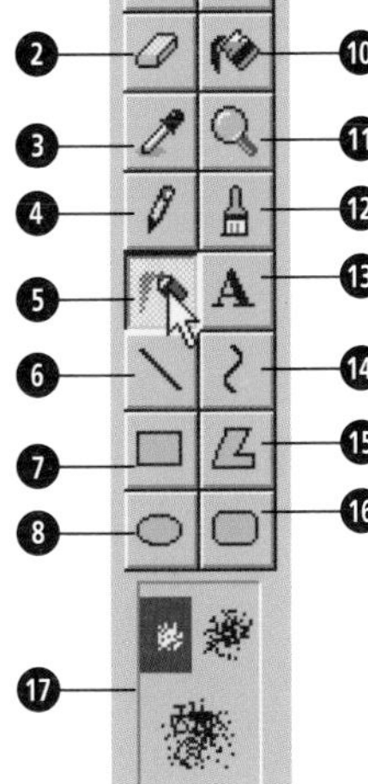

PAINT TOOLS

1. Free-Form Select
2. Eraser/Color Eraser
3. Pick Color
4. Pencil
5. Airbrush
6. Line
7. Rectangle
8. Ellipse
9. Select
10. Fill With Color
11. Magnifier
12. Brush
13. Text
14. Curve
15. Polygon
16. Rounded Rectangle
17. Airbrush Nozzles

Note: The Airbrush Nozzles Palette only shows when the Airbrush tool is selected.

Find Out More...
We have only been able to give an overview of Paint here. The **Help** drop-down menu within the program contains numerous hints and tips for greater creativity.

IMAGING

Windows Imaging is a great application for scanning or importing images and downloading photographs directly from a digital camera. Notes can be added to images and then the whole document can be printed out or emailed.

QUICK AND FUN

- Imaging is very simple to use, and yet it offers countless opportunities for creating documents that you can share with family and friends with its direct email link.
- If you have a scanner connected to your computer, then images can be instantly placed in an imaging document and printed out.
- Text can be added to documents as well as to images in a variety of entertaining ways.
- Documents can be created to your own specifications. You can choose the file type that you require, the level of color needed (whether a single color or millions of colors), decide whether you want to compress your document to save disk space or time while sending by email, and select the resolution and size of your image.

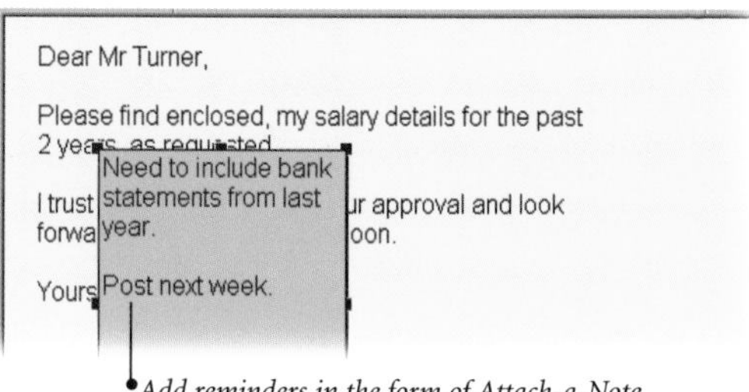

Add reminders in the form of Attach-a-Note

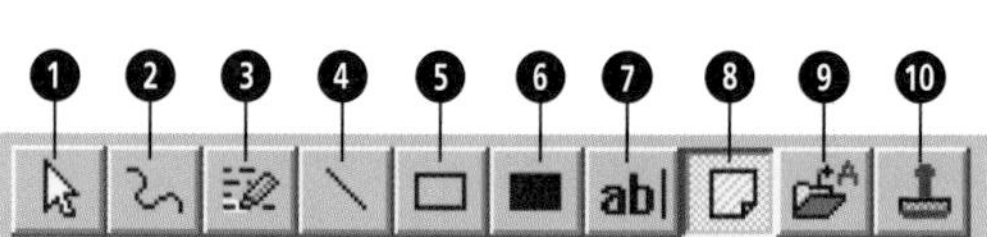

IMAGING TOOLS

❶ Annotation Selection
Selects annotation for deleting, moving, or changing

❷ Freehand Line
Draw a freehand line, and change its color and width

❸ Highlighter
Use this to highlight important areas of text

❹ Straight Line
Draw a straight line

❺ Hollow Rectangle
Change the width of the rectangle's line and add color

❻ Filled Rectangle
Draw a solid rectangle

❼ Text
Type and edit text and select different fonts

❽ Attach-a-Note
Place a sticky note, change its color and its font style

❾ Text From File
Import text from a file

❿ Rubber Stamp
Place a rubber stamp effect on your page. You can even create your own designs.

WORDPAD

Wordpad takes text editing further than Notepad. With Wordpad, you are able to design and produce colorful documents, and insert graphics (as shown here) or photographs that you may have created or downloaded from the internet. You will see that Wordpad has a far more extensive range of tools than Notepad.

1 ENTERING AND SELECTING TEXT

- Wordpad, like Notepad and Paint, is opened from the **Start** menu, moving to **Programs**, choosing **Accessories**, and then **Wordpad.**
- When you start typing into the document that opens, a font size of 10 points is used automatically. However, the font size can be reduced or enlarged.
- Hold down the mouse button when the cursor is at the end of the line, then drag the cursor over the text to highlight the line.

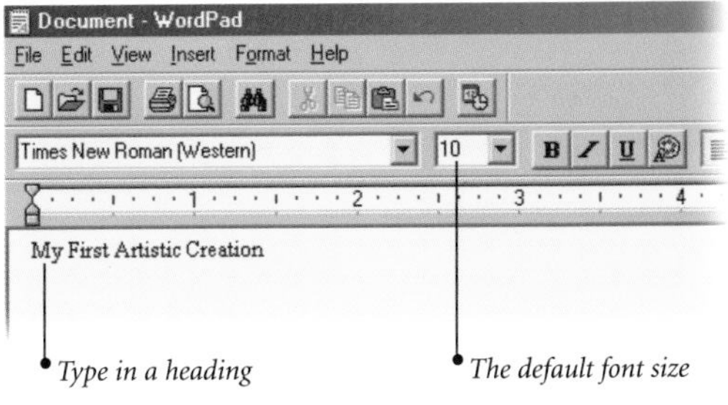

Type in a heading

The default font size

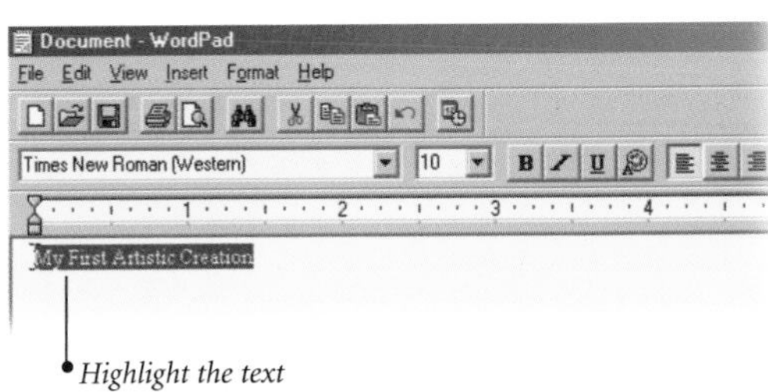

Highlight the text

2 SELECTING THE FONT SIZE

- Click on the down arrow to the right of the Font Size box, and in the drop-down menu click on a larger font size. Here, a font size of 22 is selected.

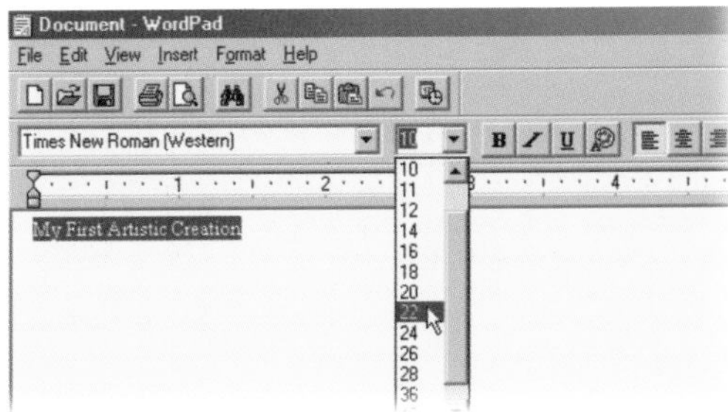

20 **Launching Notepad**

- The text changes to the selected size.
- Click the cursor at the end of the line of text to deselect it, and press Enter ↵ twice.

The cursor is now here

3 INSERTING AN OBJECT

- Click on **Insert** in the Menu bar and click on **Object** in the drop-down menu that appears.

*Click on **Object***

4 BROWSING FOR AN IMAGE

- The **Insert Object** dialog box opens. As the image to be inserted is in a file, click on the **Create from File** radio button.

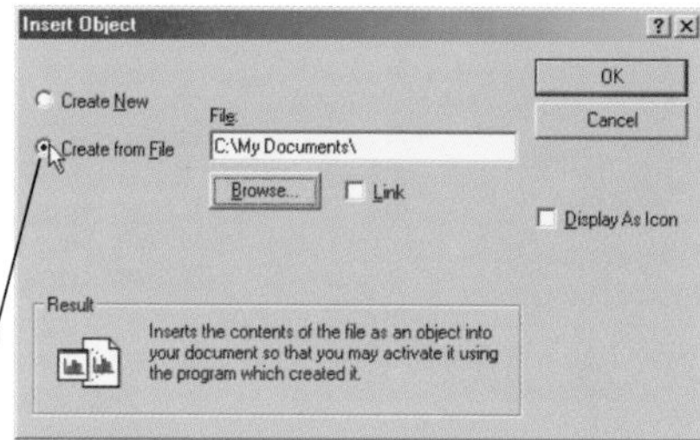

*Click on **Create from File***

- The contents of the dialog box change to show a text field where the names of folders and files can be displayed.
- Click on the **Browse** button to navigate to the location of the graphic.

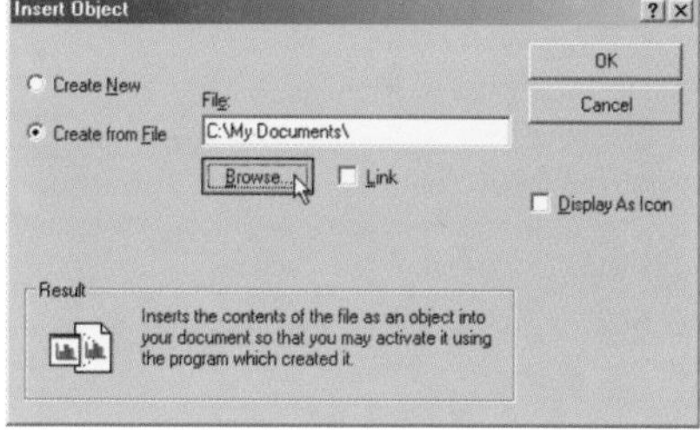

5 OPENING MY PICTURES

- The **Browse** dialog box opens. The image of the tree, which was created using Paint, is stored in the **My Pictures** folder.
- Double-click on that folder to open it.

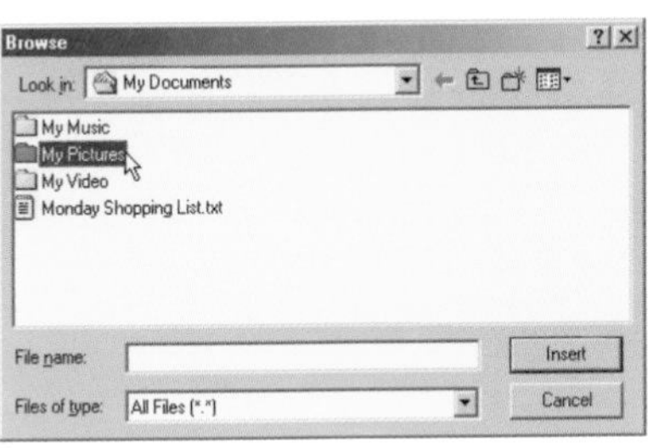

6 SELECTING THE IMAGE

- The tree is the only image contained in the **My Pictures** folder.
- Click on the image and then on the **Insert** button.

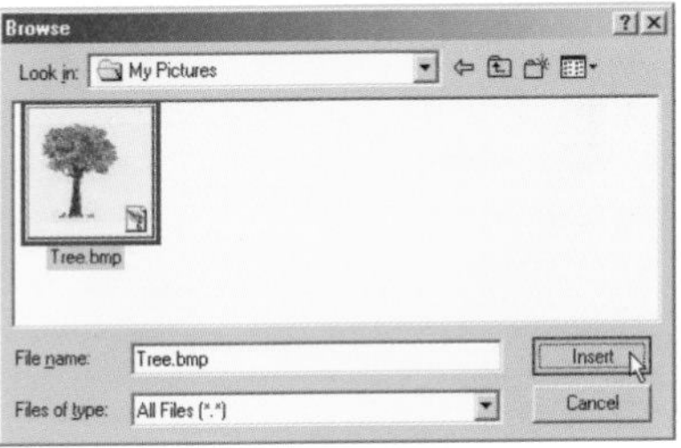

7 INSERTING THE SELECTION

- The filename is shown in the text field, and you can now click on **OK**.

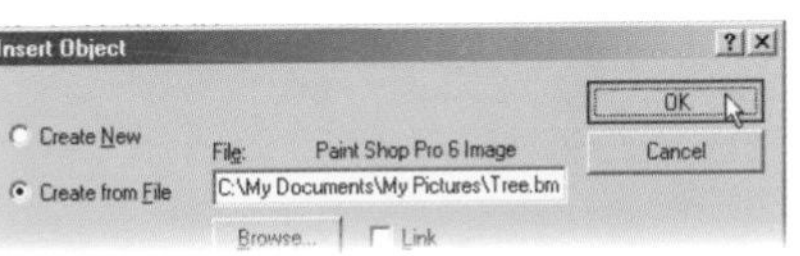

8 THE INSERTED GRAPHIC

- The picture is inserted into the document below the heading.
- The techniques shown here can be used for a variety of different purposes in different documents – from letter-heads to greeting cards.

25 **The Finished Drawing**

INSTALLING SOFTWARE

Having Windows Me installed on your computer means that you have a great many new and exciting programs to explore and play with. However, the time will come when you will want to develop and expand your computing and gaming horizons. This means that you will want to start to installing software.

WHERE CAN YOU OBTAIN SOFTWARE?

There are many ways to source software, and thousands of applications are available – from the latest games to a program to help redesign your backyard.

Where you look for software depends on what you want. Large graphics-creation programs are available from computer stores and an immense range of mail-order websites. Computer utilities are available as downloads or from CDs on the covers of computer magazines.

Websites are a useful source of free software.

WHAT DIFFERENT FORMS OF SOFTWARE ARE AVAILABLE?

The bulk of the software you will install is the commercially available form that you install on one computer and make one backup copy . Another form of software is shareware, which you can try before paying a fee to use it. After a trial period, you are then asked to pay a registration fee, which is less than you would pay for commercial software, and which funds the author to support the software, update it, and develop new programs. In some cases, you may receive updates and manuals.

A NOTE OF CAUTION

Installing software is far from being a completely safe operation. New programs can have the tendency to want to work in parts of your computer where other programs are working, which can lead to conflicts. Programs might also try to install themselves in the system tray at the right-hand end of the taskbar, which should be reserved for programs that need to be running all the time, such as antivirus software. The most important precaution you can take is to monitor each installation closely. Read what each window says, and if it's unclear or unwanted, just click on the "No" option.

35 The Problem of Software Piracy

INSTALLING FROM A CD

For this example, a piece of software is going to be installed from a CD-ROM that was supplied with a popular home computing magazine. These discs can contain fully functional programs or trial versions with a limited life.

1 AUTORUN FEATURE

● Most CDs that are free with magazines have an autorun feature that automatically opens the CD-ROM when it is placed in the drive.
● A screen appears that usually lists the software available and advertisements for other products.

2 CHOOSING YOUR SOFTWARE

● Choose the program that you want to install. In this case, we are going to install the latest version of WinZip, which is a file-archive and compression utility.
● After clicking on the **Install Software** button, the setup begins.

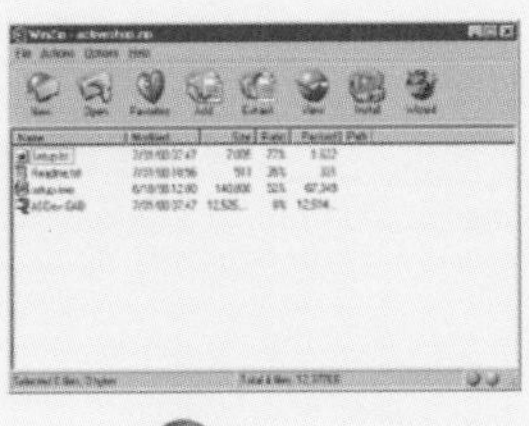

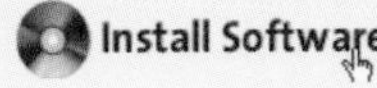

WHAT IS FILE COMPRESSION?

WinZip – as we have mentioned – is a file compression and archiving utility. File compression is a method of making files smaller in size, and therefore saving disk space, without losing quality or data, which is vital for files you want to archive. WinZip is probably the most common program used for this function. A trial version of WinZip can be downloaded from the internet from its own website: **http://www.winzip.com**.

- The **WinZip Setup** window appears.
- Click on the **Setup** button to continue.

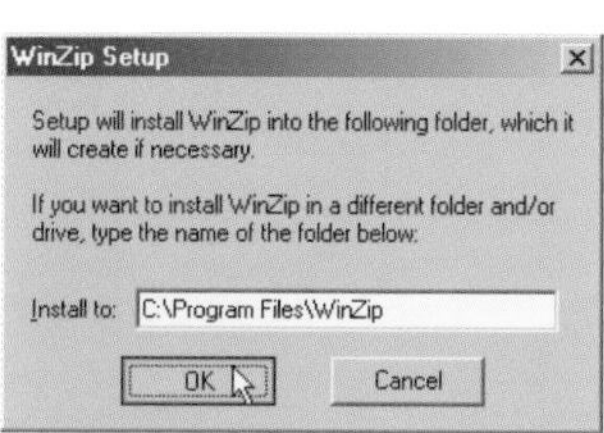

3 CHOOSING A LOCATION

- Programs usually install themselves in a location that they select, and to which you can agree by clicking on **OK**.

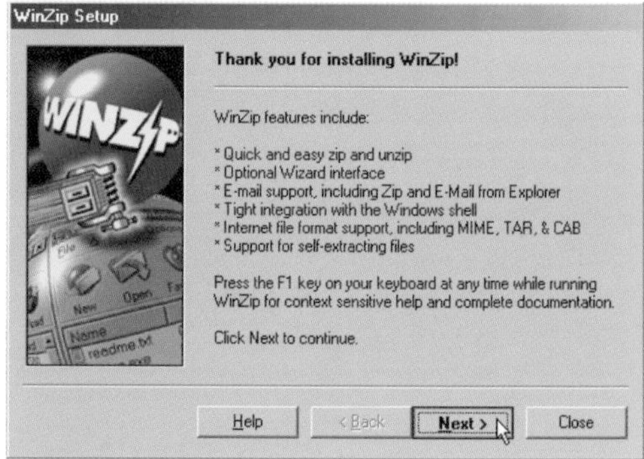

- A screen appears, providing information on the software you are about to install.
- After reading the information, click on **Next** to continue.

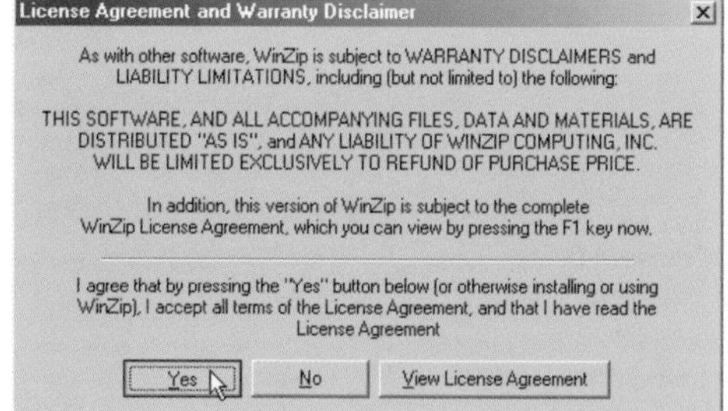

4 LICENSE AGREEMENT

- The License Agreement is where the lawyers briefly take over from the programmers. Some applications present you with the whole agreement. WinZip's option is simpler where you can simply click on **Yes** to agree.

License Agreement and Warranty Disclaimer

As with other software, WinZip is subject to WARRANTY DISCLAIMERS and LIABILITY LIMITATIONS, including (but not limited to) the following:

THIS SOFTWARE, AND ALL ACCOMPANYING FILES, DATA AND MATERIALS, ARE DISTRIBUTED "AS IS", and ANY LIABILITY OF WINZIP COMPUTING, INC. WILL BE LIMITED EXCLUSIVELY TO REFUND OF PURCHASE PRICE.

In addition, this version of WinZip is subject to the complete WinZip License Agreement, which you can view by pressing the F1 key now.

I agree that by pressing the "Yes" button below (or otherwise installing or using WinZip), I accept all terms of the License Agreement, and that I have read the License Agreement

Yes | No | View License Agreement

5 CONTINUING INSTALLING

- You are offered the opportunity to print or view useful information about the installation and the use of WinZip.
- Click **Next** to continue with the installation.

- WinZip has almost completed its installation. It now needs to know which type of WinZip you wish to start with. In this example, we have chosen to start with WinZip Classic. Read the text on the dialog box carefully and make your own choice.

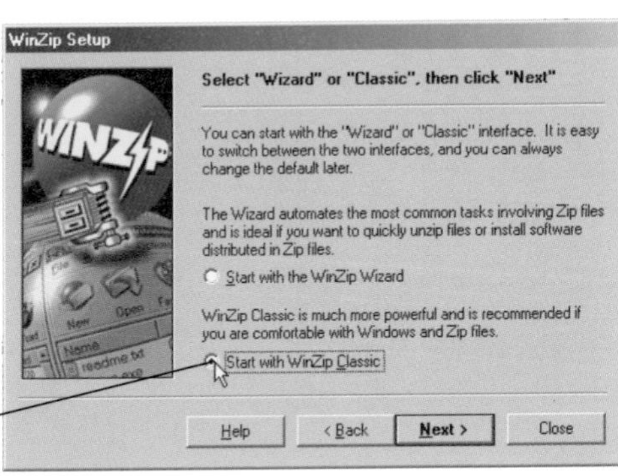

We have chosen to start with WinZip Classic

- When you are given the choice, click in the circle (known as a "radio button") next to **Start with WinZip Classic.** Don't be deterred by the fact that this is recommended for people already familiar with Zip files – you will not be performing any tasks within the program yet.
- Click on **Next.**

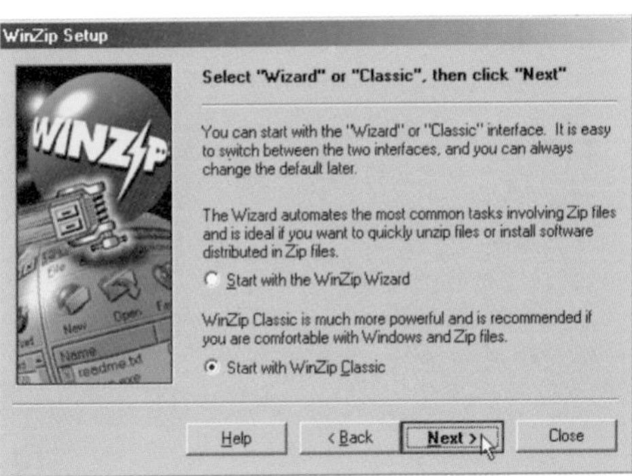

● Click in the radio button next to **Express setup (recommended)**.
● Click on the **Next** button.

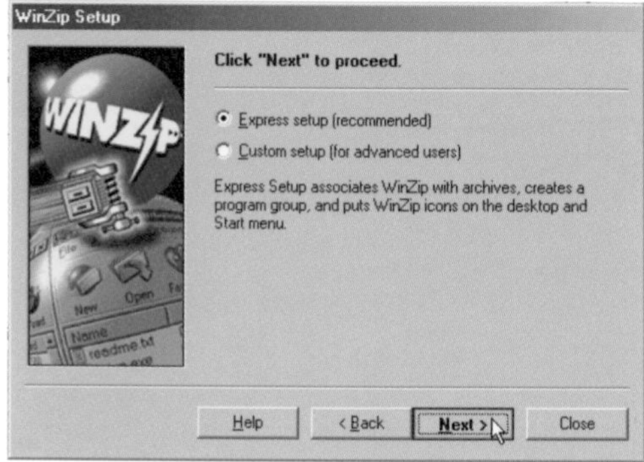

● Once the installation process is complete, click on the **Finish** button.

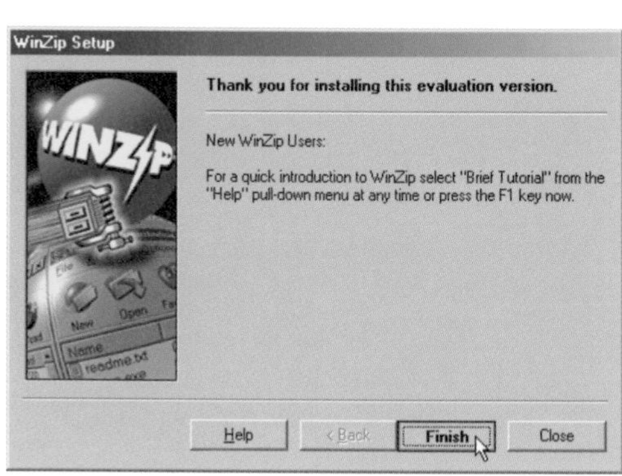

6 CLOSING WINZIP

● You can now close the the program by clicking on the **Close** button.
● In future, WinZip will automatically expand compressed files when you download them to your computer.

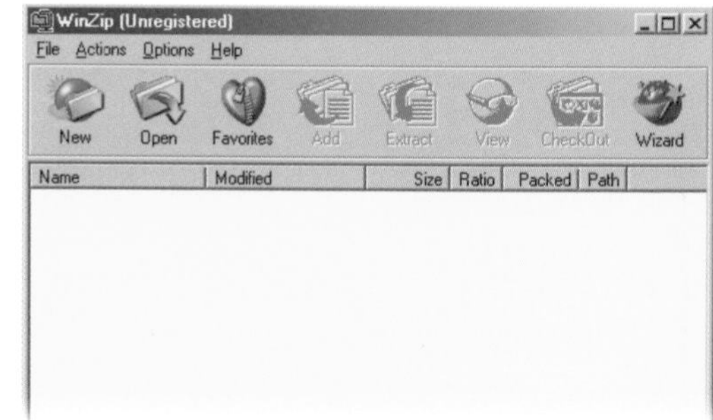

● As well as installing the software on your computer, other changes have been made. A shortcut to WinZip has automatically been placed on the desktop.

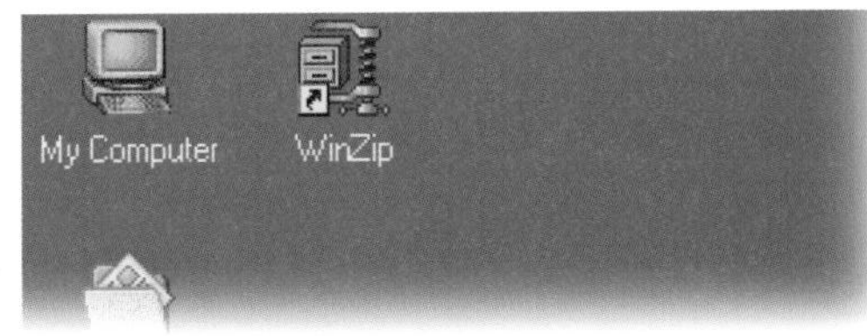

● In addition, the **Start** menu now also contains a shortcut to WinZip.

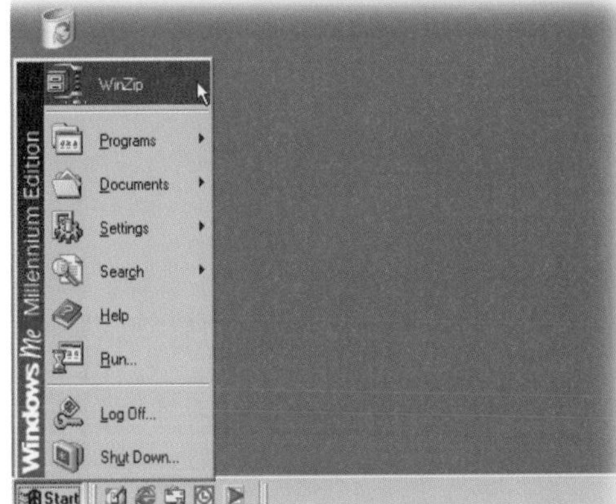

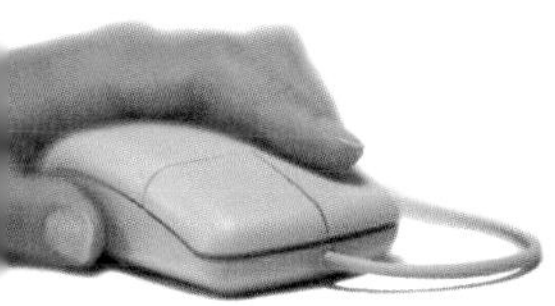

THE PROBLEM OF SOFTWARE PIRACY

● The ease with which computer software can be copied from computer to computer makes it very tempting to copy programs for friends. However, when you buy a program, you are buying a license to install the program only on one computer and to make a backup copy for archiving purposes only. Any use of computer software beyond those activities is illegal.

● In the US, the Copyright Act gives the copyright owner the exclusive rights to reproduce the work and distribute copies. Buying software does not include the purchase of those legal rights of reproduction and distribution as well.

● In addition to being illegal, software piracy is very risky. The computer from which the software is copied may contain a virus that is also copied. The version may not be fully functional, and it will not have manuals or technical support. Neither is there access to patches, upgrades, or innovations. Piracy also deprives the software manufacturers of their legitimate earnings.

FILES AND FOLDERS

The more you use your PC, the more files and folders you will create. These need to kept in a structured way to reduce the possibility of forgetting where, or what, they are.

MANAGING FOLDERS AND FILES

The two key features for successfully managing your files and folders are how you store them and how you name them. Good storage is grouping by type, and folders can be stored in other folders to create related subgroups. Naming files and folders is simply labeling them – the clearer the label, the clearer the contents.

1 CREATING A NEW FOLDER

- Creating a new folder is the starting point for making a collection of documents.
- Windows Me provides a starting point for storing your files and folders by placing the **My Documents** folder on the desktop. Double-clicking on the folder opens the **My Documents** window.
- Click on **File** in the Menu bar, place the cursor over **New** to display the submenu and click on **Folder**.
- A new folder appears alongside the existing folders in the **My Documents** window.

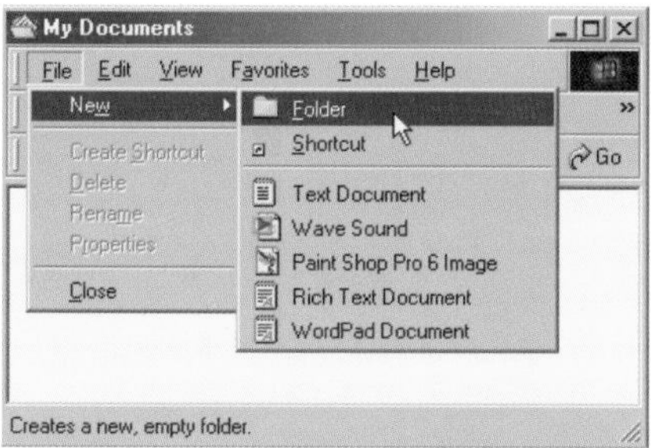

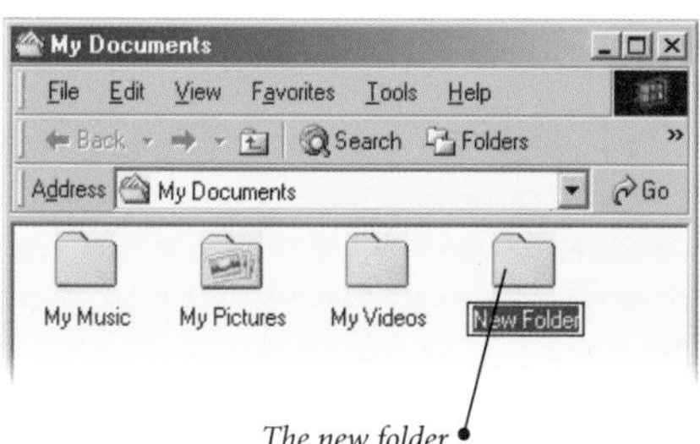

The new folder

2 NAMING THE NEW FOLDER

- With the new folder highlighted, type in the new name: **Letters**. Press the Enter key and deselect the folder by clicking once in any blank area of the window.

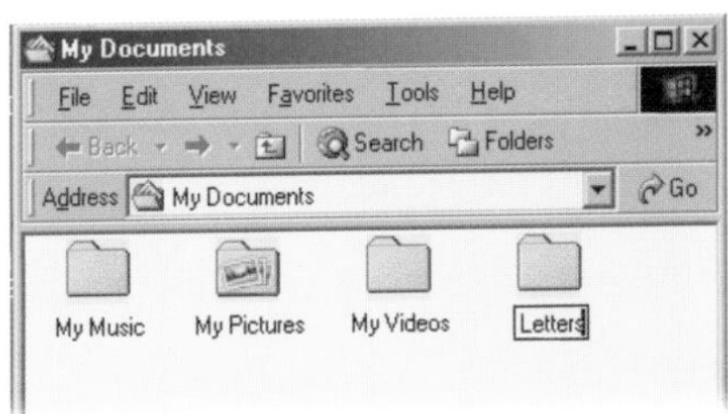

3 MAKING FOLDERS WITHIN A FOLDER

- Double-click on the new **Letters** folder to open its window.
- In this window, create folders with names relating to their intended contents, for example, **Aunt Daisy**, **Bank Manager**, and **Work**.

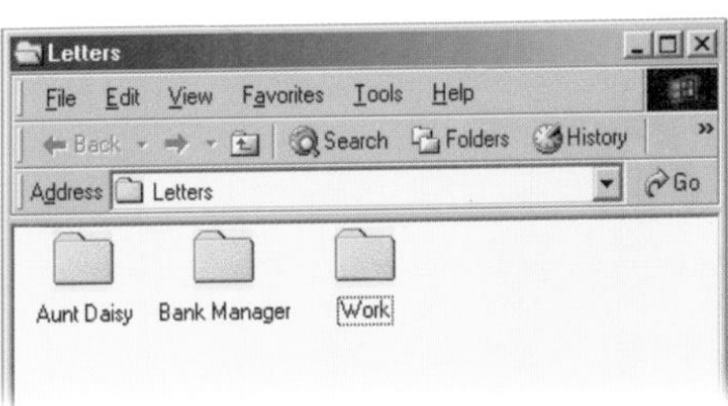

MOVING A FILE BETWEEN LOCATIONS

As you use your computer more, you are likely to create collections of files, possibly by using the software referred to earlier. Eventually, your first folders will need revising, and you will need to move files. Moving a file involves selecting the file, displaying the destination folder, and moving the file to that location.

1 OPENING THE FOLDER

- Open the folder containing the file that is to be moved.
- In this case, the **Work** folder has been opened, and the file to be moved is **Freelance Records**.

20 **Windows Me Programs**

2 CHOOSING THE NEW LOCATION

- The new location for this file is a new folder that has been created and named **Freelance Work**.
- Open the new **Freelance Work** folder by double-clicking on it.

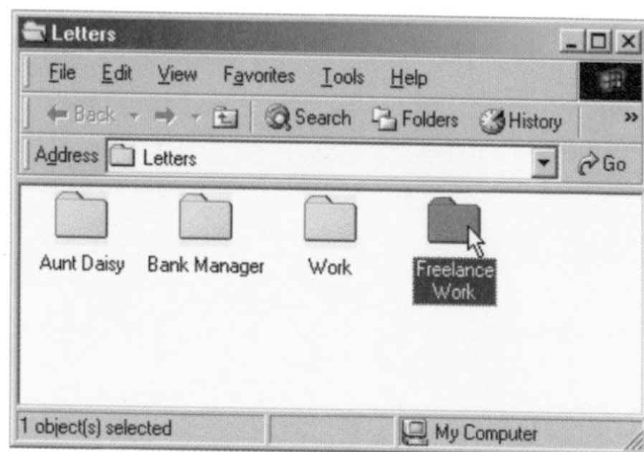

3 ARRANGING THE WINDOWS

- Close the **Letters** folder by clicking on its **Close** button. Move the cursor over any empty area of the taskbar and click the right-hand mouse button.
- Select the **Tile Windows Vertically** option from the pop-up menu.

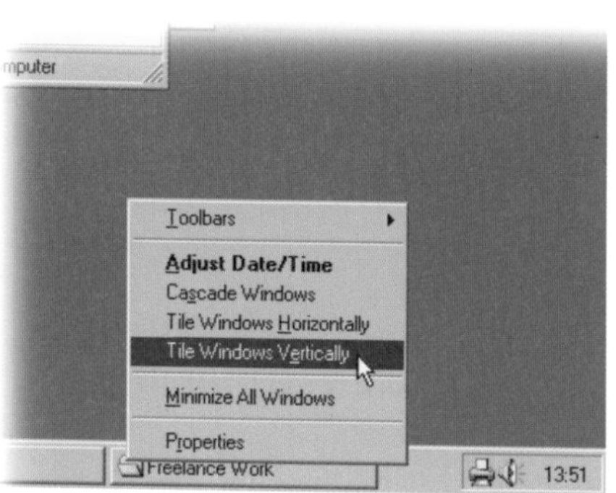

FILE AND FOLDER SELECTION TECHNIQUES

THREE METHODS OF SELECTION

- Irrespective of whether you are copying, moving, or deleting files or folders, there are three selection techniques for items that you want to work on. You can select files or folders individually, select groups of items, or select items that are separated.

SELECTING A SINGLE FILE OR FOLDER

- This technique is the simplest of the three. Any individual folder or file can be selected simply by clicking on it.

SELECTING ADJACENT FILES OR FOLDERS

- To select several adjacent items, select the first one as you would a single item. Move the mouse cursor over the next item, hold down the Shift key, and left-click. Both items are selected and further items can be selected in the same way.

SELECTING SEPARATE FILES OR FOLDERS

- Hold down the Ctrl key before clicking on each separate item.

12 Minimizing and Maximizing Individual Windows

4 MOVING THE FILES

- The two windows appear alongside each other. Select the file that you are going to move and, while holding down the left mouse button, drag the outline of the file to the new location.

- When the cursor is over the window of the new folder, release the mouse button. The file disappears from the first window and reappears in the second.

USING THE RIGHT MOUSE BUTTON OPTIONS

- Once you become familiar with copying and moving folders and files, you will feel confident about using the many shortcuts that Windows Me provides.
- One set of shortcuts is available through the right mouse button. Choose a folder or file to copy or move, place the cursor over it, hold down the right mouse button, and drag the folder or file to another folder or window.
- When you release the mouse button, this pop-up menu appears, allowing you to select the appropriate action.

COPYING FILES TO OTHER LOCATIONS

Copying a file is similar to moving a file, except that the original remains in place and a copy is placed in a new location on your computer. Files can also be copied to a floppy disk as a backup to use if the original file is damaged or lost, or to copy a file to a computer that does not have internet, email, or network access.

1 CHOOSING THE FILE TO COPY

- Here we are building up the contents of a folder called **Accountant**, which will be sent at the end of the tax year. The file **Freelance Records** needs to be copied to this folder.
- The first step is to open the two folders in question: **Freelance Work** and **Accountant**.

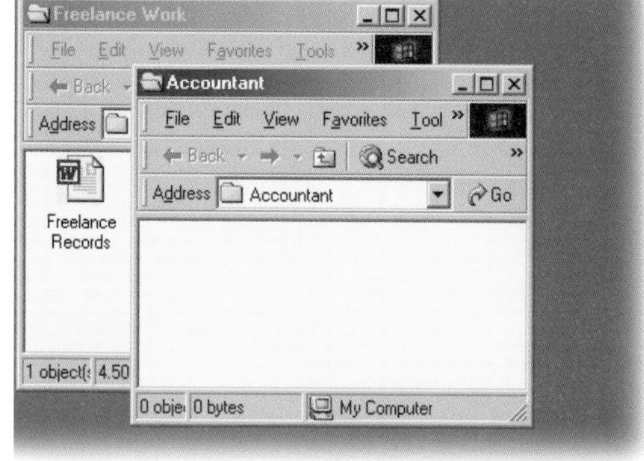

2 DRAGGING THE FILE

- After using the **Tile Windows Vertically** command, select the file to be copied by clicking on it. Hold down the Ctrl key as you drag the file. A plus (+) sign follows the outline, indicating an additional version is being created.

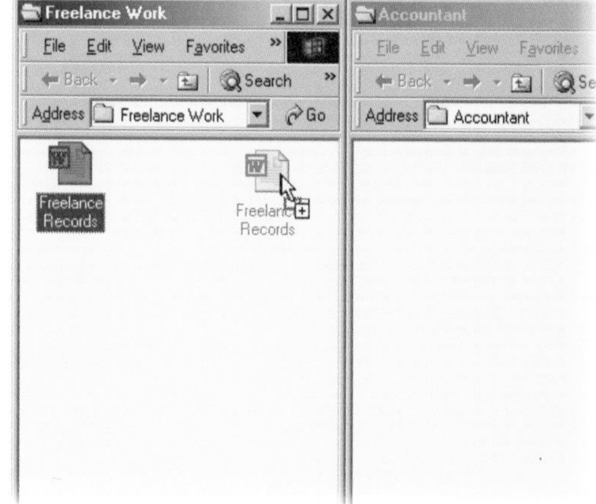

38 Arranging the Windows

3 PLACING THE FILE

● Release the mouse button when the file icon is over the second window. A duplicate of the file appears in the window, leaving the original file in place.

DELETING UNWANTED FILES

When you start out with a new computer and a hard drive with what appears to be a colossal capacity, it's very easy to create countless files without any apparent consequences. Although your hard drive may not become full, it will eventually become unmanageable – and deleting old files then becomes an important option.

SELECTING THE FILE OR FOLDER

● There are three ways to delete files and folders in Windows Me. In this example, we are deleting a folder. This action also deletes the files that the folder contains, so ensure that none of the files in the folder is needed.

● The first step is to select the file or folder.

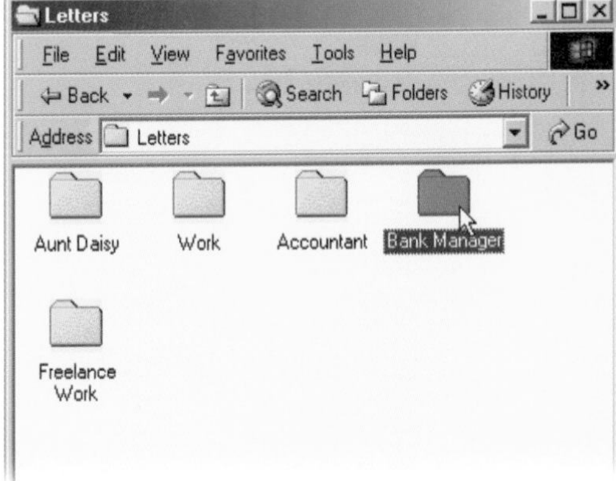

DELETING BY MENU

- The first method of deleting an item is to click on the **File** menu and select **Delete** from the menu.
- An alert box appears asking you to confirm that you want to delete the item, simply click on **Yes**.

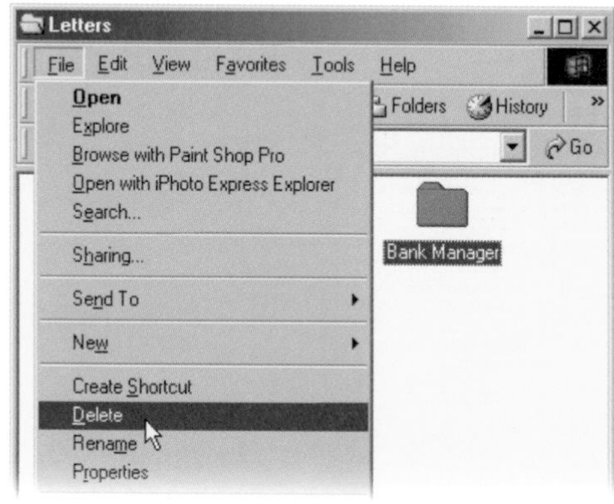

DELETING BY RIGHT-CLICKING

- Placing the cursor over the item to be deleted and click with the right mouse button. A pop-up menu of options appears onscreen.
- This menu contains many of the most frequently used activities. Clicking on **Delete** opens the alert box again.

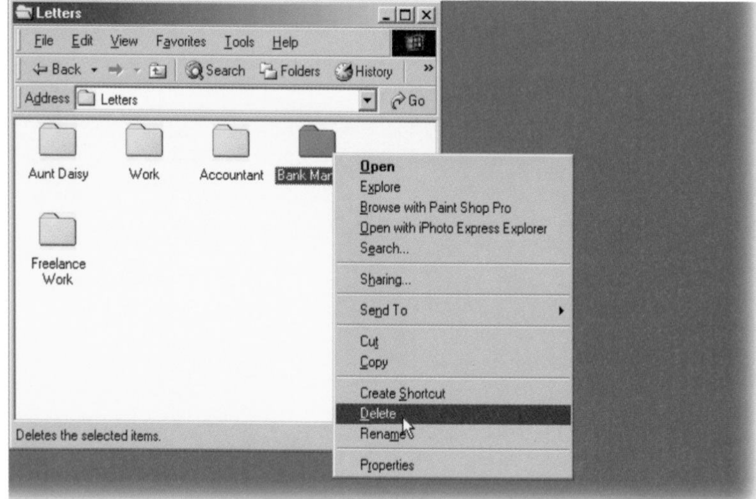

DELETING BY DRAGGING

- The previous two methods move the item to the **Recycle Bin**. The third method is simply to drag the item directly to the Bin.
- Place the cursor over the item, hold down the left mouse button, and drag it to the **Recycle Bin**. Then release the mouse button. No alert box appears asking you to confirm this action.

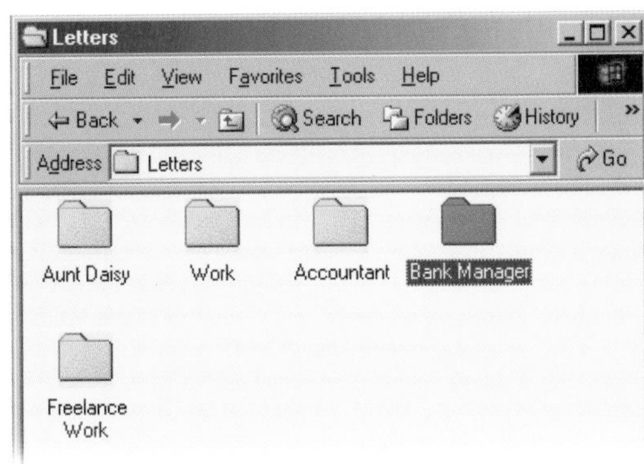

OPENING THE RECYCLE BIN

- In the early stages of using Windows Me, it's worth checking the contents of the **Recycle Bin** before emptying it.
- To open the Bin, double-click on it.

VIEWING THE BIN'S CONTENTS

- The **Recycle Bin** window opens and displays the files you have thrown away since the bin was last emptied.
- Click on **File** in the Menu bar. The drop-down menu includes options either to **Empty Recycle Bin** or to **Delete**. The former permanently deletes all the contents, the latter deletes only the files you have selected.

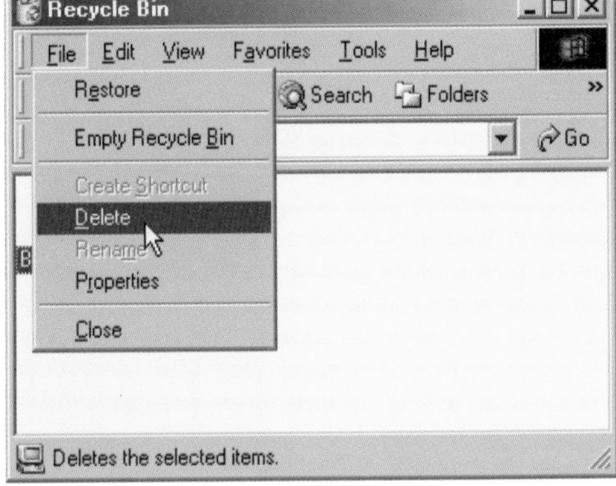

PERMANENTLY REMOVING FILES

- An alert box appears onscreen asking you to confirm the deletion. Clicking on the **Yes** button deletes either all the files or those you selected.
- The window of the **Recycle Bin** is cleared of those files. If you elected to remove all the files, the icon of the **Recycle Bin** shows that it is now empty.

RECYCLE BIN PROPERTIES

Right-click on the **Recycle Bin** and then click on **Properties** in the pop-up menu. In the **Recycle Bin Properties** dialog box, you can prevent the **Confirm File Delete** box from appearing. You can also remove files without first sending them to the Bin.

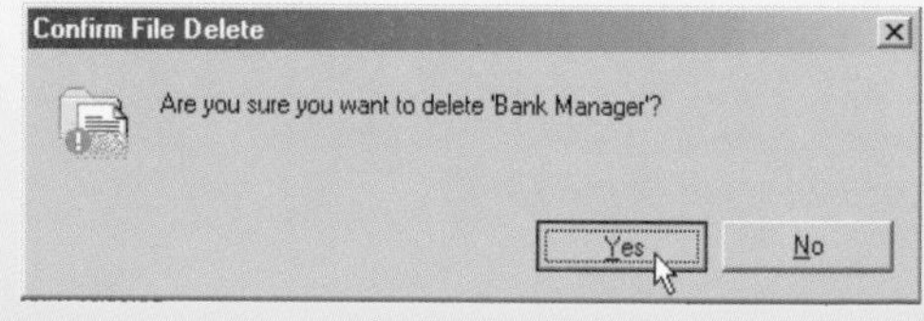

VIEWING FILES IN WINDOWS EXPLORER

Windows Explorer provides another means of viewing and managing your files. In addition to all the normal windows functions, Windows Explorer shows you the location of a file in terms of the hierarchy of folders on your hard drive.

1 LAUNCHING EXPLORER

- Click once on the **Start** button in the bottom left corner of the taskbar.
- Choose **Programs** from the pop-up menu, move to **Accessories**, and select **Windows Explorer** from the submenu that opens.

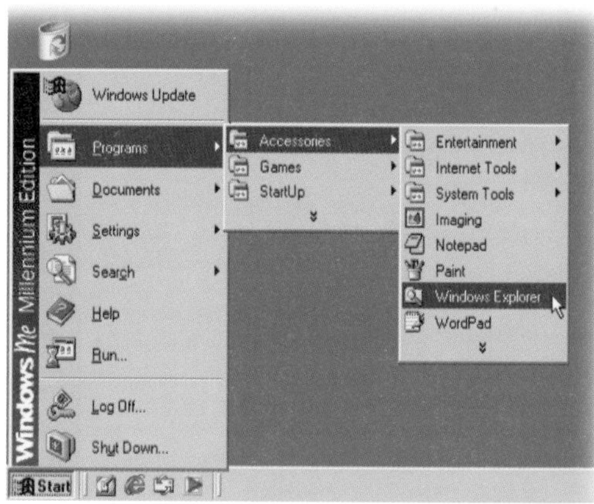

2 THE EXPLORER WINDOW

- The window opens. It consists of two panels.
- The left-hand panel shows the hierarchy of the different parts of your computer and the folders that it contains. By default, items branch down from the **Desktop** – the top level of your computer.
- The right-hand panel of the Explorer Window displays the contents of the folder or component that is highlighted in the left-hand panel.

Many options appear as buttons in a menu bar

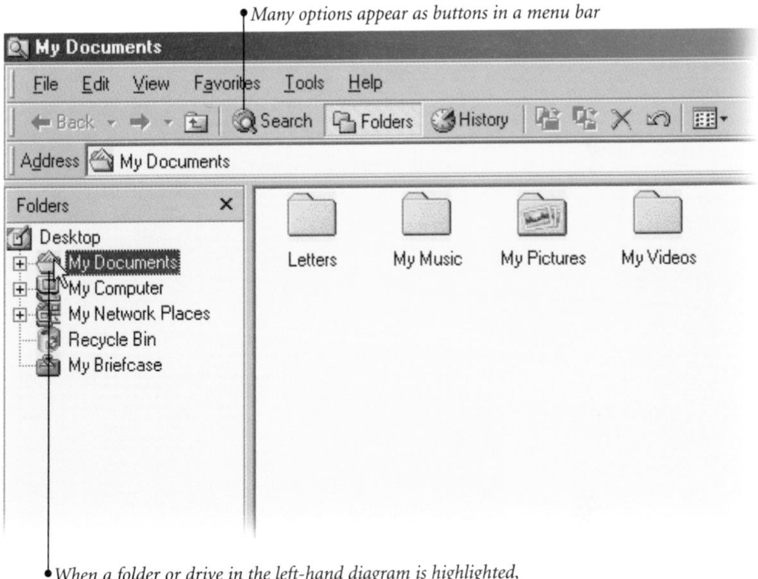

When a folder or drive in the left-hand diagram is highlighted, the files and folders it contains appear in the panel on the right

TIPS FOR WINDOWS EXPLORER

- Quick-launch Windows Explorer by holding down the [Shift] key and double-clicking on the **My Computer** icon.
- Undo the moving of a file by clicking the **Undo** button in the Windows Explorer toolbar.
- Move back up the hierarchy of folders displayed in Windows Explorer by pressing the [← Bksp] key.
- Optimize the column widths in the right-hand panel of Explorer by holding down the [Ctrl] key and pressing the + key at the right-hand end of the keyboard.

RESIZING THE WINDOW PANELS

● In order to see a wider area of the folders and components that are displayed in the left-hand panel, place the cursor over the gray vertical bar that divides the two parts of the window. The cursor changes to a double-headed arrow.
● Hold down the left mouse button and drag the bar to the right.
● When the left-hand panel shows sufficient detail, release the left mouse button.

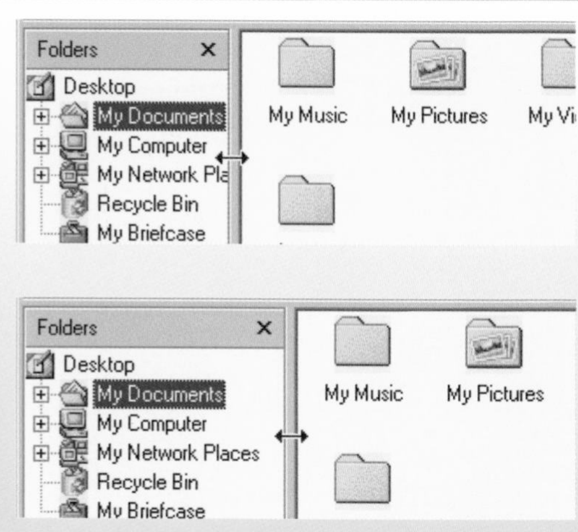

3 REVEALING THE FOLDERS

● Position the cursor over one of the squares in the window that contains a plus sign (+) and left-click once. In this case, the plus sign selected is the one next to the **My Documents** folder.
● A list of folders is displayed, branching down and to the right of the selected folder. The plus sign (+) changes to a minus sign (–), indicating that the contents list can be closed by clicking on that sign.

4 REVEALING THE FOLDER LIST

• Clicking on the plus sign (+) next to the **Letters** folder now produces a list below it of the folders that it contains – starting with **Accountant** and ending with **Work**.

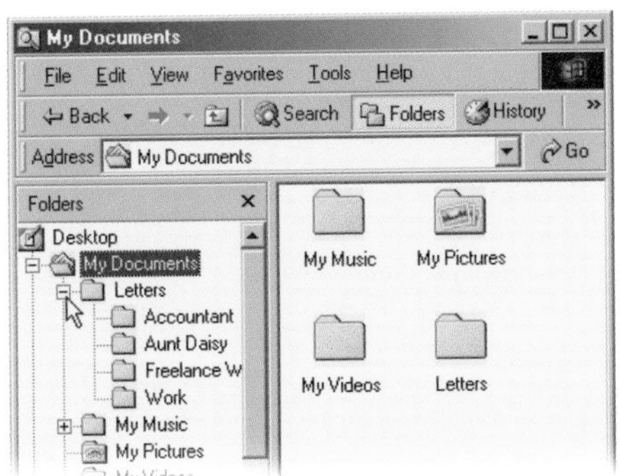

5 REVEALING THE FOLDERS

• If you click on the **Letters** folder icon, you will see the folders that it contains displayed in the right-hand panel of the Windows Explorer window.

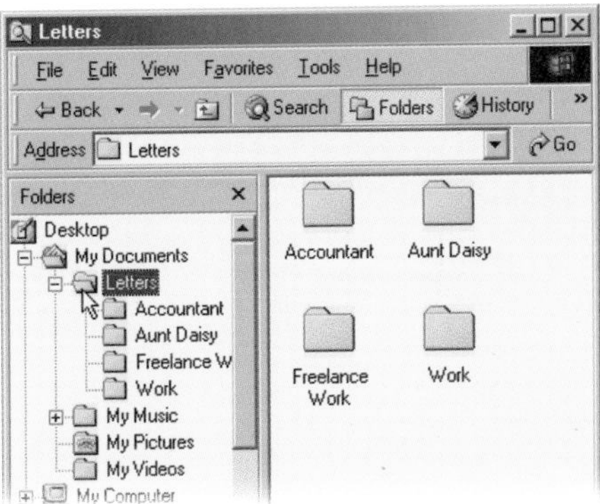

6 REVEALING THE FILES INSIDE

• Finally, click on the folder named **Accountant**. The file, **Freelance Records**, which was copied into it earlier, is shown in the right-hand panel and lies at the end of the hierarchical structure of folders and files.

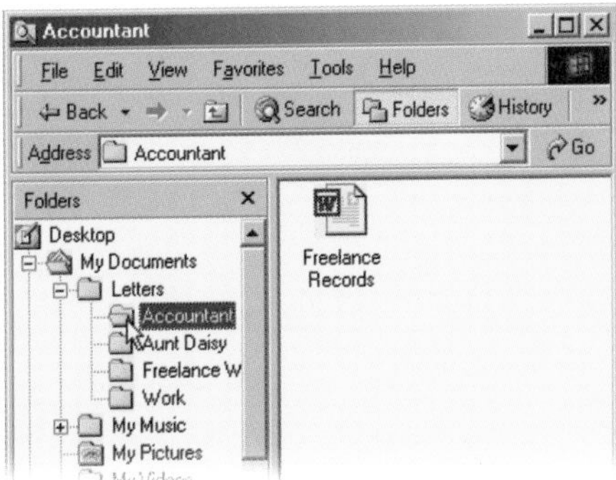

INTERNET AND EMAIL

A few years ago, the idea that people around the world would soon be talking, shopping, and working by using the internet and email appeared far-fetched indeed.

GETTING CONNECTED

Windows Me makes it very easy to connect to the internet through wizard-driven help screens. Once connected, you can launch Internet Explorer, known as your "internet browser," to log on at the start of each session on the internet.

WHAT YOU WILL NEED

Internet Explorer is there to let you browse the world wide web, but there are a couple of extra items that are needed before you can connect. Most modern PCs will have an internal modem installed, but you will also need a telephone cable connected to this. The other end of the cable needs to be attached to the telephone line. Sometimes, internet users have a second line installed at home. It can be very frustrating trying to call a person who is constantly engaged because they are surfing the internet!

This site offers links to a plethora of subjects. Each of the links contains its own links.

WHAT'S ON THE INTERNET?

Perhaps the question should really be, "What isn't on the internet?"

Whether you are using it for research on American Transcendentalism and need details on the life and works of Emerson, or whether you need details on the latest space launch from Cape Canaveral, the answers will be online. Text and images can be selected and pasted into Wordpad for later use. Pages can be bookmarked for revisiting at a later date, and you may even build a website of your own where you can share your news and views.

THE INTERNET CONNECTION WIZARD

The first time that you use Internet Explorer, you will be presented with the Internet Connection Wizard. This will help you to set up a new internet account and should make getting online a pain-free experience. By default, your homepage and the first website that you see will be Microsoft's site (**MSN.com**).

CONNECTION WIZARD

- Double-click on the **Internet Explorer** icon on the desktop.
- The **Internet Connection Wizard** opens. By default, the **I want to sign up for a new Internet account...** radio button is selected.
- From this point on, follow the sequence of the Internet Connection Wizard's screens, and you will establish your internet connection.

Internet Service Provider (ISP)

The Internet Connection Wizard will put you in touch with an ISP. An ISP provides your gateway to the internet, with a local telephone number that gives you access to its servers.

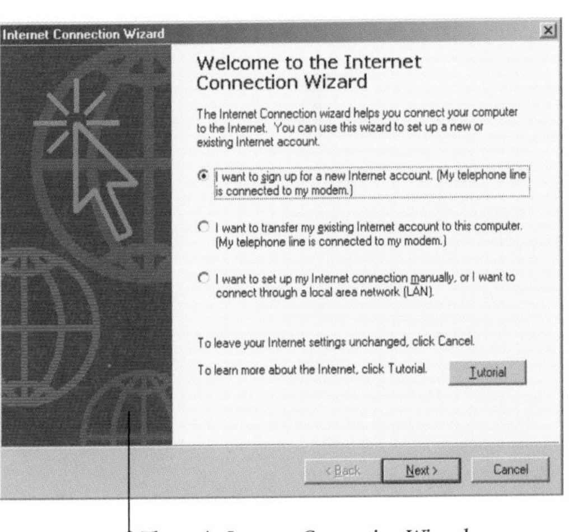

The main ***Internet Connection Wizard*** *screen*

OTHER WAYS TO CONNECT

The Internet Connection Wizard can be opened via its own menu entry. Click on the **Start** button, select **Accessories**, move to **Communications**, and select **Internet Connection Wizard.**

INTERNET EXPLORER

Internet Explorer heads a suite of programs produced by Microsoft dedicated to everything internet-related, from browsing the web, to writing and sending emails, to building and publishing your own web pages. Internet Explorer is called a web browser; the other well-known browser is Netscape Navigator.

WHAT DOES EXPLORER DO?

Internet Explorer is the web-browsing program that enables you to connect to websites and view them, surf the web using hypertext links, and download (copy) files from the internet to your own computer. By default, its email features operate through Outlook Express.

SEARCH WITH INTERNET EXPLORER

Now that you are connected to the internet, it is time to discover just what Internet Explorer can do. It may seem a little daunting at first as there seems to be a bewildering number of buttons and drop-down menus. However, you can navigate the internet with Explorer by using a small number of buttons.

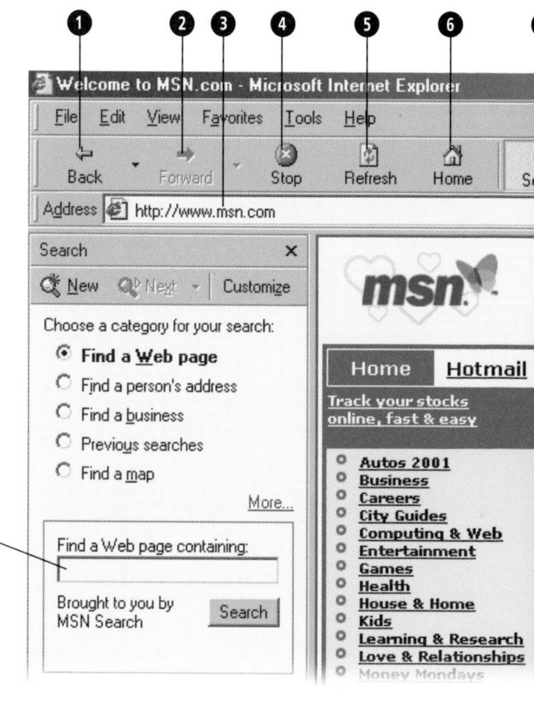

*Type in a keyword here, and then click on the **Search** button below to start viewing a website; note that there are other options for obtaining different search results by clicking in one of the radio buttons above*

THE STANDARD TOOLBAR

❶ Back
❷ Forward
The Back and Forward buttons take you through the web pages you have visited.
❸ Address bar
Enter the address of a website and go directly to that site.
❹ Stop
Stops a page downloading.
❺ Refresh
Refreshes the current page.
❻ Home
Loads the default home page.
❼ Search
Opens the Search panel in the Explorer window. This gives you access to features that help you connect to search engines.
❽ Favorites
Save, access, and manage your favorite sites on the web.
❾ History
Opens the History panel.
❿ Mail
Provides a menu of options related to email.
⓫ Print
Prints the current page.
⓬ Edit
Edit and save a version of the current web page.
⓭ Messenger
Stay in touch with your friends by finding out who's online and sending messages.

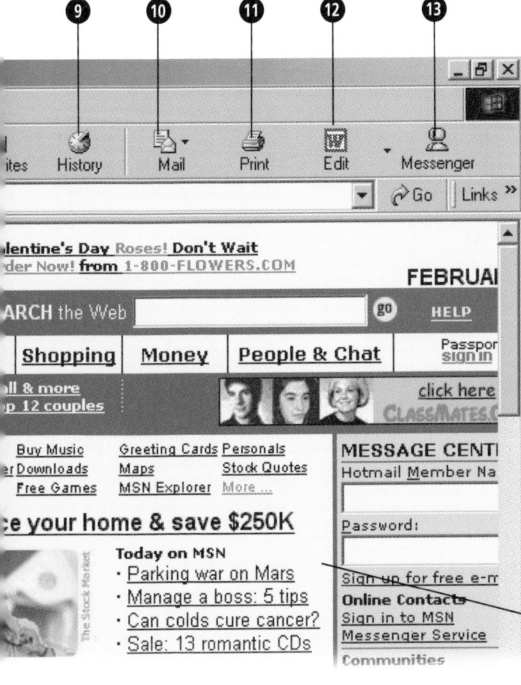

www.msn.com
The website shown here, **www.msn. com**, is Microsoft's main website. Each of the links down the left-hand side opens up a page containing hundreds of links to other pages related to that topic.

This is the main window where everything that you choose to view is displayed

GETTING ONLINE HELP AND SUPPORT

Windows Me **Help and Support** is an invaluable source of answers to questions that will help you make the most of your computer. You can take tours that provide overviews of given topics, follow step-by-step instructions to achieve a desired result, find troubleshooting tips, and link to the internet for up-to-date information.

1 HELP BY TOPIC

- Clicking on **Help** in the **Start** menu opens the **Help and Support** center.
- Choose a topic that you require further information on, or type a keyword in the **Search** panel to have Windows look for you.

Windows Me Millennium
Settings
Search
Help
Run...
Log Off
Shut Down...
Start

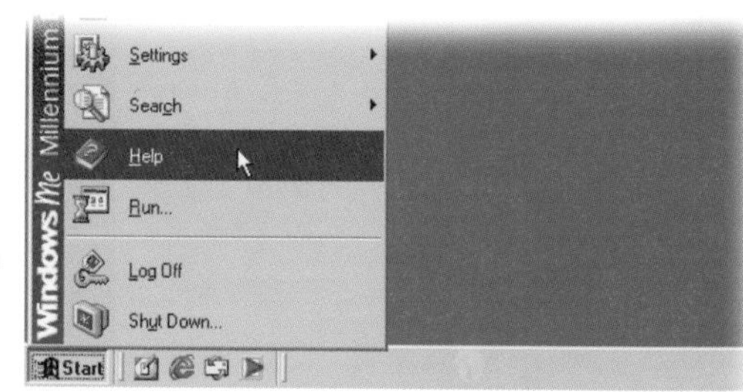

Select a help topic from the list

Or type in a keyword here

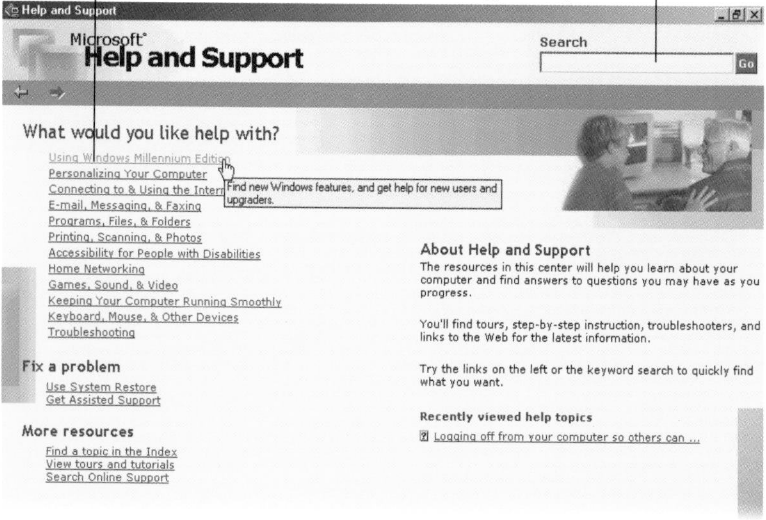

Help and Support
Microsoft Help and Support
Search
Go
What would you like help with?
Using Windows Millennium Edition
Personalizing Your Computer
Connecting to & Using the Internet
E-mail, Messaging, & Faxing
Programs, Files, & Folders
Printing, Scanning, & Photos
Accessibility for People with Disabilities
Home Networking
Games, Sound, & Video
Keeping Your Computer Running Smoothly
Keyboard, Mouse, & Other Devices
Troubleshooting
Find new Windows features, and get help for new users and upgraders.
Fix a problem
Use System Restore
Get Assisted Support
More resources
Find a topic in the Index
View tours and tutorials
Search Online Support
About Help and Support
The resources in this center will help you learn about your computer and find answers to questions you may have as you progress.
You'll find tours, step-by-step instruction, troubleshooters, and links to the Web for the latest information.
Try the links on the left or the keyword search to quickly find what you want.
Recently viewed help topics
Logging off from your computer so others can ...

2 TYPE IN THE KEYWORD

● In this example, we have typed the keyword **Music** into the **Search** field.
● Click on the **Go** button.

3 THE SEARCH RESULTS

● As you can see, there is an astonishing number of results returned. Clicking on one of the topics will take you to that subject.

Using the index

An alternative method of finding help on the subject area that's puzzling you is to click on **Find a topic in the Index** where you can then enter the precise term describing what you need help with.

4 NARROWING THE SEARCH

● Once a topic has been selected, the right-hand panel narrows the results further. Clicking on one of these titles will now take you directly to the help that is available on that subject.

MICROSOFT OUTLOOK EXPRESS

Email is simply the electronic equivalent of the postal service. From your address, you send mail to your ISP [49], which sends the mail via the worldwide network of servers to the recipient's ISP, from which he or she can get mail addressed to them.

EMAIL

Outlook Express is an application for sending, receiving, and managing your email. It has the facility for storing all your email addresses and personal contact details in an electronic address book, which is easy to edit and keep up-to-date.

With Outlook Express, you can send and receive emails that contain, not only text elements, but also images, separate documents, and links to websites that you want to share with friends. Images and documents can easily be sent as "attachments" that the recipient can open and view.

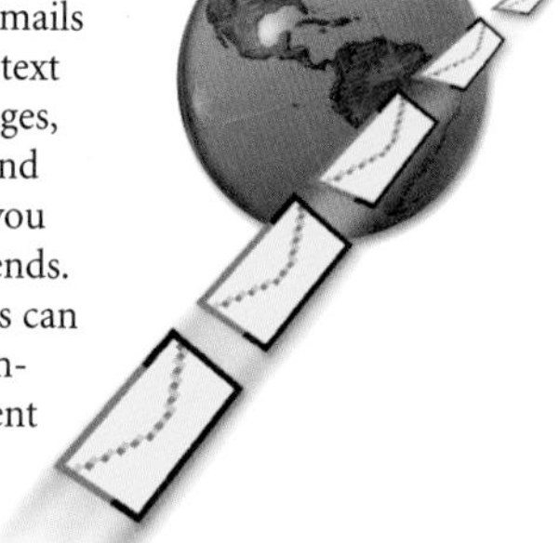

THE ELEMENTS THAT MAKE UP AN EMAIL ADDRESS

When you signed up with your ISP, you will have been asked to give details for your email address. This address is unique to you and is made up from several pieces of information, including your name and country code.

❶ User Name
Identifies the addressee.

❷ Separator
An @ ("at") symbol separates the user and domain names.

❸ Domain name
The computer address, with dots (periods) as separators.

❹ Country code
All countries except the US use a two-letter suffix as the last part of the address. For example, uk stands for the United Kingdom, il for Israel, and nz for New Zealand.

49 **Internet Service Provider (ISP)**

LAUNCHING OUTLOOK EXPRESS

You can launch the application, Outlook Express, in three principal ways: from the Windows Start Menu, from the Windows desktop (if the Outlook Express shortcut is there), or from within Microsoft Internet Explorer itself.

FROM THE START MENU

• To launch Outlook Express from the Start menu, click on the **Start** button, move up to **Programs**, and select **Outlook Express** from the submenu.

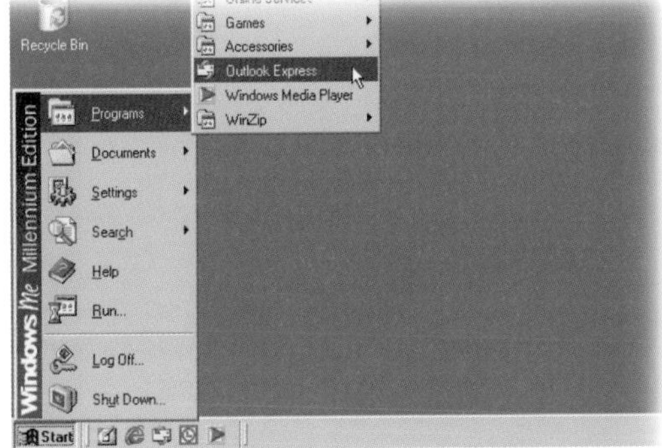

FROM THE DESKTOP

• To launch Outlook Express from the desktop, locate the **Outlook Express** shortcut icon and double-click on it with the left mouse button.

FROM INTERNET EXPLORER

• Open Internet Explorer and click on the **Mail** button on the main toolbar.
• Select the option that you require from the drop-down menu.
• Outlook Express is launched, showing either a new message window or the **Inbox**, depending on the option that you selected from the menu.

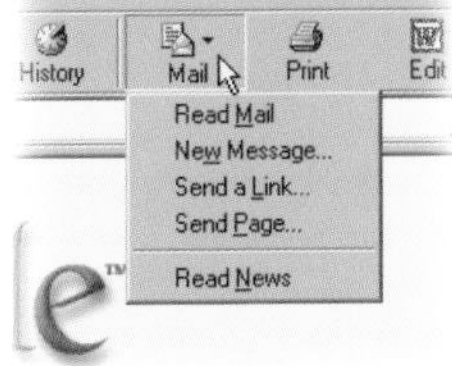

THE OUTLOOK EXPRESS WINDOW

The Outlook Express window is divided into different sections, some of which are visible only when you perform the actions they relate to. You can personalize the Outlook Express window to display as many of these elements as you wish.

WINDOW PANELS

❶ Outlook bar
The Outlook bar provides handy shortcuts to some of the key folders. You can customize the Outlook bar to include the folders that you use most frequently.

❷ Contacts panel
This panel displays a list of all the contacts that are stored in the current user's Address Book.

❸ Folders panel
A folder can be selected in this panel to become the currently active folder whose contents are displayed in the main area of the window.

❹ Folders list
This shows all the folders and subfolders in which the current user's email and newsgroup messages have been saved.

❺ Views bar
The Views bar allows you to show or hide different categories of messages according to your choice.

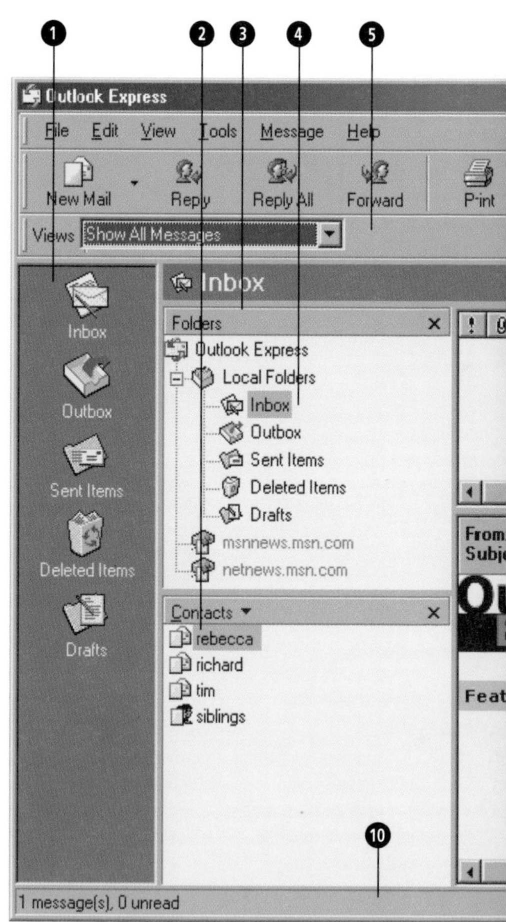

THE MENU BAR

The menu bar at the top of the screen, just below the title bar, contains menu options, such as **File** and **Edit**, that are shared with other Microsoft programs and may be familiar. However, the **Message** option, through which messages are controlled, is unique to Outlook Express.

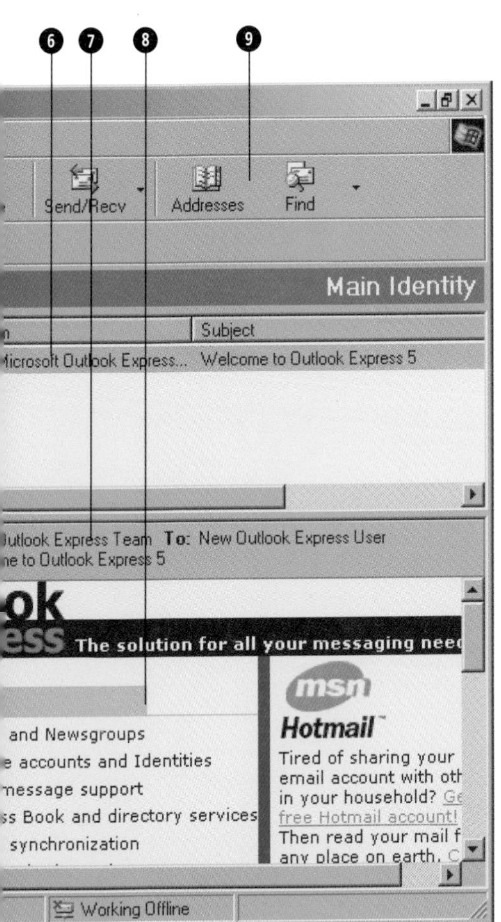

WINDOW PANELS

❻ Message list
This shows a list of all the messages that are contained in the active folder (the folder that has been selected from the Folder list or Outlook bar).

❼ Preview panel header
Contains summary information about the currently selected message.

❽ Preview panel
The contents of the selected message in the Message list can be read here.

❾ Toolbar
The bar at the top of your screen displays buttons that enable you to access Outlook's main features quickly and easily. The items on the toolbar change depending on which part of the program you are using.

❿ Status bar
Displays information about activities that you perform and the status of your internet connection.

The Message Window

Once the **New Mail** button has been clicked on the toolbar, an email can be composed in the Message window. Email messages are made from several parts. The message header contains the sender's and the recipient's address details, and the subject of the message. The message body contains the message itself. A message may also contain other elements, such as file attachments.

COMPOSING A NEW MESSAGE

- Select a mail folder, such as the **Inbox**, by clicking on it in the Folder list or Outlook bar.
- Click the **New Mail** button on the toolbar. This opens a new Outlook Express message window.
- Click the left mouse button in the message body area of the window and type in the text of your message.
- Address the message.
- Add any file attachments to send with the message.
- Send the message.

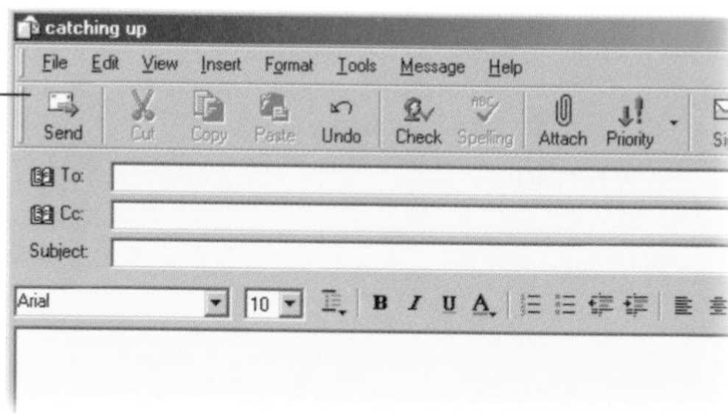

*When you have finished composing your message and have addressed the mail, click on the **Send** button.*

THE MESSAGE WINDOW

❶ The To: field
This contains the email address of the recipient of the message. Every message must contain the address.

❷ The Cc: field
This contains the email addresses of people to whom you would like to send "carbon copies" of the message.

❸ The Subject: field
This contains the subject of the message. Filling in the subject is optional, but it is good practice to use a subject so that people can tell at a glance what your message is about.

❹ Message Body
This is where you type the text of the message. It acts as a normal word-processing window.

❺ Toolbar
This provides access to the main activities you will want to carry out when typing a message. There are buttons for editing text (cut, copy, and paste); for checking spelling; and for sending and prioritizing the message when it is finished.

❻ Formatting Toolbar
This offers some of the standard word-processing features to enable you to align text, choose the font and style, manage paragraphs, and add bullet points. Formatting can only be applied to text that has been selected (by clicking and dragging the mouse). Not all email programs have the sophisticated word-processing features that Outlook Express contains. If you do not know which program the addressee has on their computer, it is advisable not to add complex formatting to your email message because their email program may not have the facilities to display it.

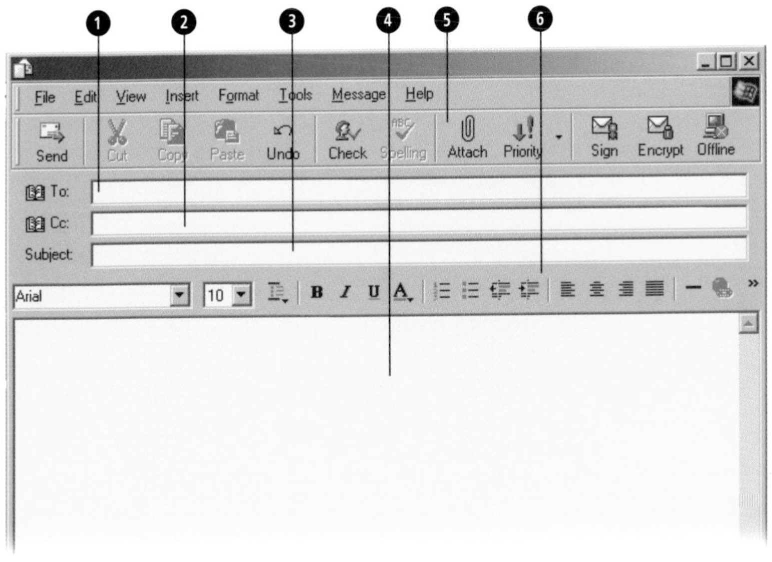

FUN AND GAMES

As you do your day's work, or complete that letter to the bank manager, Windows Me can offer some light relief, whether playing CDs, listening to internet radio, or watching movies.

THE MULTIMEDIA EXPERIENCE

Possibly the biggest change between Windows Me and previous Windows versions is the collection of facilities contained in Windows Me for managing digital media files. Here we look at Windows Media Player for Windows Me, which encompasses all the latest audio/visual technology in one package, including playing a music CD. We look at customizing Media Player and using the visualizer. We also examine the Explorer radio bar and playing Me games.

LAUNCHING MEDIA PLAYER

- You can use Media Player to play audio CDs, video/animation files, and also to control items such as the CD-ROM drive.
- Media Player can be accessed from the **Start** menu or the Quick Launch section of the taskbar.
- Note that when nothing is playing on Media Player, some of the options and buttons are inaccessible.

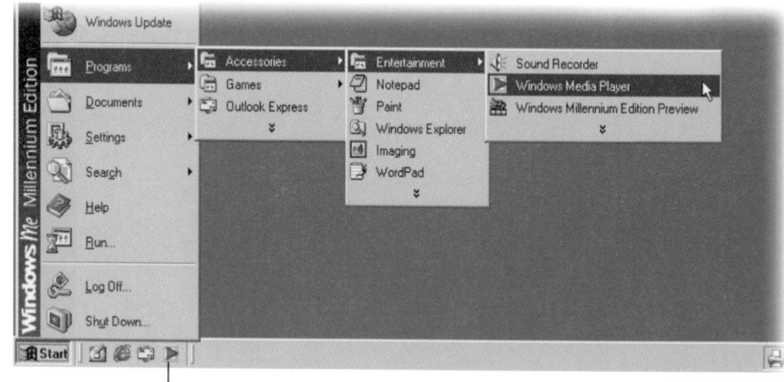

Windows Media Player Quick Launch icon

THE MEDIA PLAYER WINDOW

To enjoy Windows Media Player, you will need a sound card, a modem, and speakers attached to your computer. Most modern computers include all these items as standard, but if you have an older PC, you may have to purchase one of these.

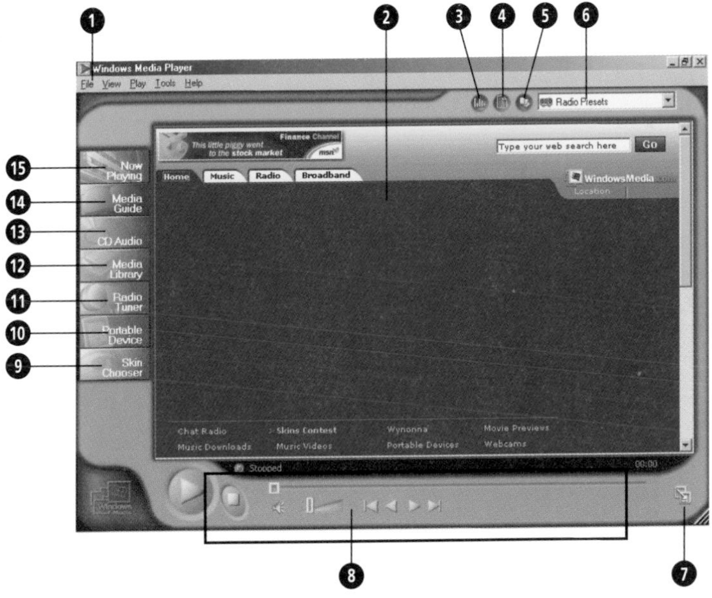

MEDIA PLAYER TOOLS

❶ Drop-down menus
❷ Main visual window
❸ Hide/show equalizer & settings *Only operable if **Now Playing** button is selected*
❹ Hide/show playlist *Only operable if **Now Playing** button is selected*
❺ Shuffle
❻ Audio selector
❼ Compact/full mode *Reduce/enlarge the size of Media Player*
❽ Audio/video controls *Not operable when there is no audio available*
❾ Skin Chooser
❿ Portable Device
⓫ Radio Tuner
⓬ Media Library
⓭ CD Audio
⓮ Media Guide
⓯ Now Playing

PLAYING A MUSIC CD

When you insert an audio CD into the CD-ROM drive on your computer, Media Player automatically detects it and starts playing immediately. When an audio CD starts playing, there are some visual changes to Media Player.

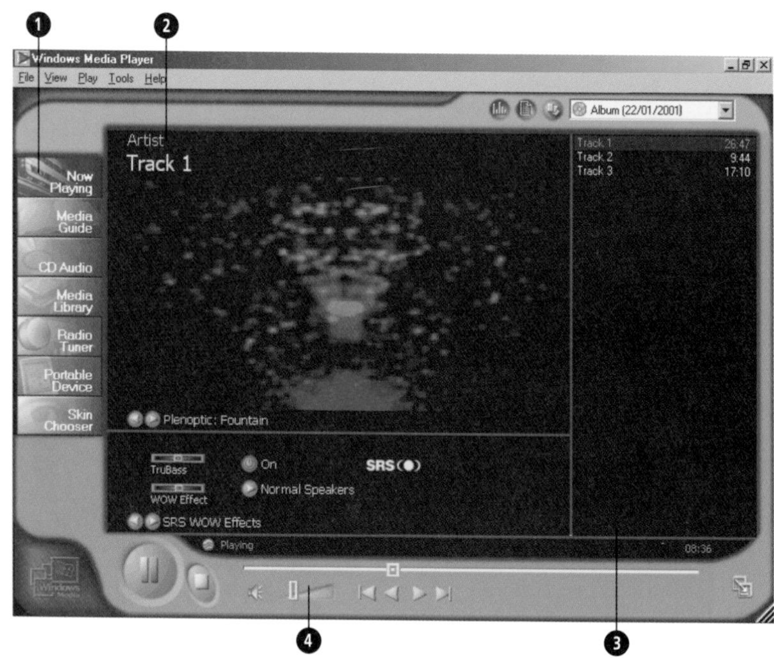

MEDIA PLAYER TOOLS

1 Now Playing button
The Now Playing button becomes highlighted when an audio CD is inserted.

2 Main visual window
The main visual window contains a "visualization" of colored patterns, which move in response to the music. It may also show the artist and title.

3 Track details window
The right-hand window has the track listing of artist, album, and track information including track times, if known.

4 Audio/visual controls
All of the Audio/visual controls are now displayed.

WHAT ELSE CAN MEDIA PLAYER DO?

THE MUSIC MACHINE

Not only can Media Player play your CDs, it can also store the songs on your computer in Windows Media Format. This makes the files very small and means they take up very little hard disk space. In addition, if you are connected to the internet, Media Player will automatically find and retrieve the name of the artist, the title of the album, and track listings for every song that you have recorded on your PC. However, if you are not connected to the internet, you can manually enter the information. Once you have built up a collection of music, Media Player allows you to build up customized playlists that can be any length you choose. Media Player can also play and store MP3 and WAV files.

MEDIA GUIDE

With Media Guide, it is possible to download music, videos, and movie trailers via the website: **WindowsMedia.com**.

RADIO

Now you can listen to the immense variety of radio stations available from around the world with Media Player. You can choose between AM, FM, or internet-only radio.

Customizing Media Player

Even the experience of playing a music CD can be heightened by personalizing the way that Windows Media Player looks onscreen. You can change the size of the player, dress it up in an elaborate or a fun skin to change its appearance, and even select a visualization effect to suit the music or your mood.

CHANGING THE APPEARANCE

- You can alter the way that Media Player looks by changing its skin. The Player has to be displayed in full mode to do this.
- Click on the **Skin Chooser** button.

● The skin selector window opens. On the right-hand side of the window, there is an image of the skin that you are using at the moment; in this case, it is the **Default Media Player** skin. In the left-hand window, there is a list of the optional skins that are supplied with Media Player.

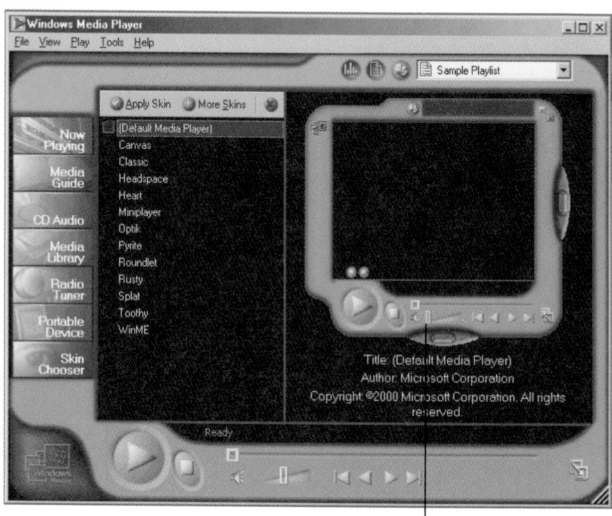

The preview window

● Clicking on each of the skin names displays a preview of the design in the right-hand window.
● Click through each of the names in turn until you find a skin that you like the look of.

Weird and wonderful, this skin is called Headspace

MORE SKINS

• If you don't like any of the optional skins that come with Media Player, **windowsmedia.com** has an immense selection of alternatives that you can browse through.
• Begin by clicking on the **More Skins** button at the top of the main Skin Chooser window.

• Your internet connection opens the **windowsmedia.com** website at the first skins page. Here you can browse through page after page of weird and wonderful skins. You can even find out what is involved in designing a skin yourself.

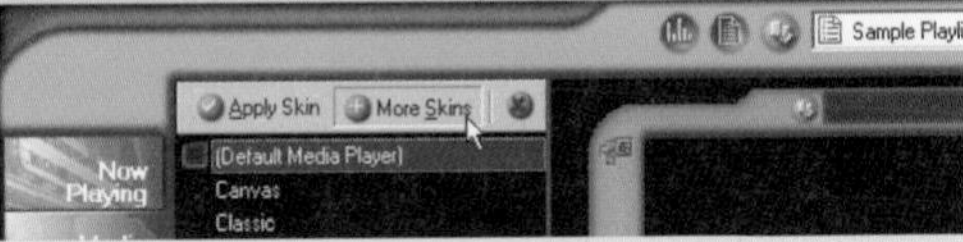

VISUALIZATIONS

Visualizations in Media Player provide a relaxing series of light shows that respond to and accompany the rhythms of the music as it plays. There are many visualizations to choose from, and they are grouped according to specific themes.

• When a CD is playing, the visualization starts, whether the player is in full or compact mode. Some skins do not have the facility to accommodate visualization, particularly in compact mode.

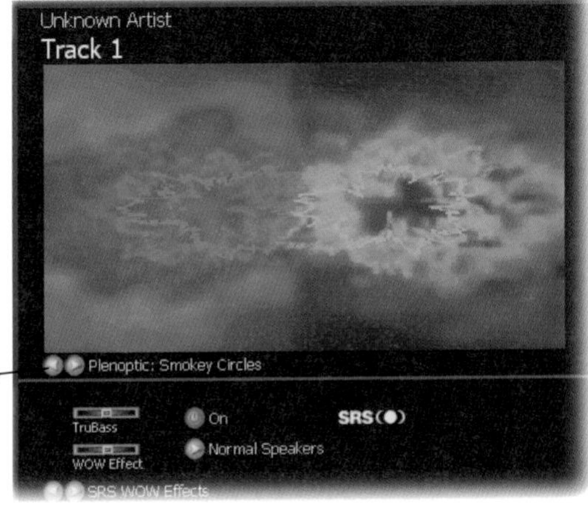

By clicking on the left and right arrows, you can scroll through the many visualization effects in Windows Media Player

Explorer Radio Bar

As well as internet-only radio stations, many national and local stations broadcast live over the internet. These will run in the background while you browse the web. Internet Explorer's Radio Guide provides links to hundreds of radio stations.

1 LOCATING THE TOOLBAR

• In the Internet Explorer window, the **Radio** toolbar can be accessed by choosing **Toolbars** from the **View** menu and then **Radio** from the drop-down menu.

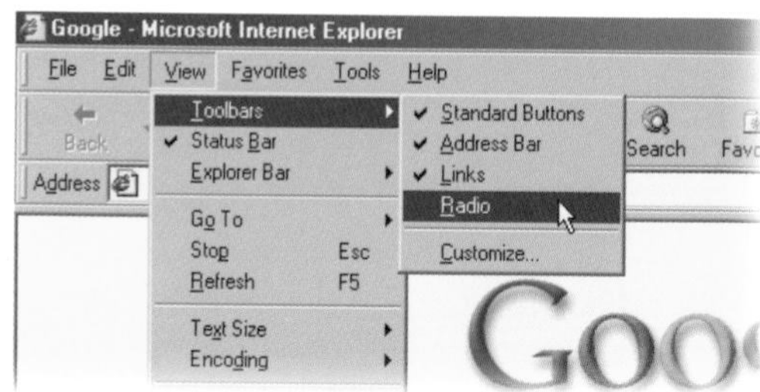

2 LOCATING THE GUIDE

• On the **Radio** toolbar, click on **Radio Stations**, and choose **Radio Station Guide** at the foot of the drop-down menu.

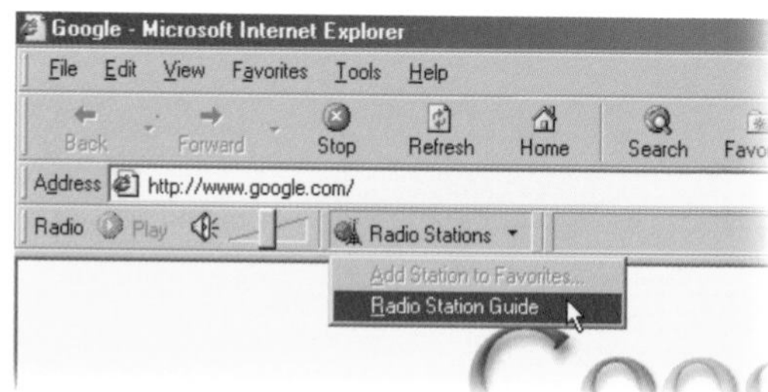

3 LOCATING THE STATIONS

• Radio stations are found by selecting a category, including **Format**, and then from subdivisions within that category.

There are many radio stations available to suit all music tastes

WINDOWS ME GAMES

Windows Me is designed to make playing games easier and faster, so after figuring out your finances or writing a letter to Aunt Dorothy, take it easy and have some fun, either playing a game solo or online against opponents anywhere in the world.

1 PLAY ON THE INTERNET

- To launch a game on the internet, begin by clicking on the **Start** button, then move to **Programs,** and then to **Games.**
- From the collection that is available in the **Games** submenu, we'll choose to play a game of **Internet Checkers.**

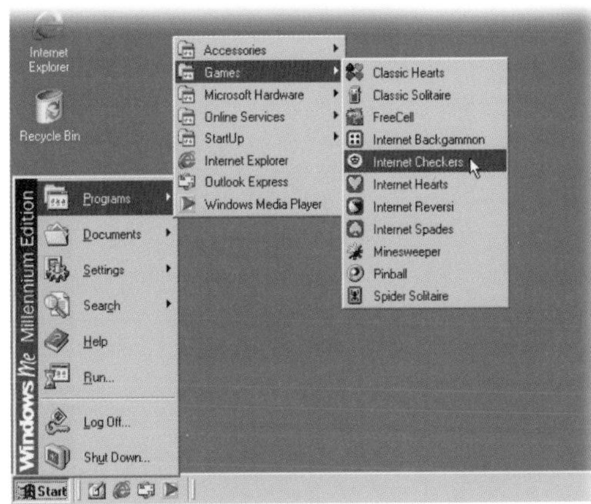

2 CONNECT TO THE INTERNET

- The first time that you play across the internet, the **Zone.com** dialog box opens onscreen.
- You can click in the **Show this every time** check box to deselect it if you don't want to see this box each time you start to play online.
- When you're ready, click on the **Play** button.

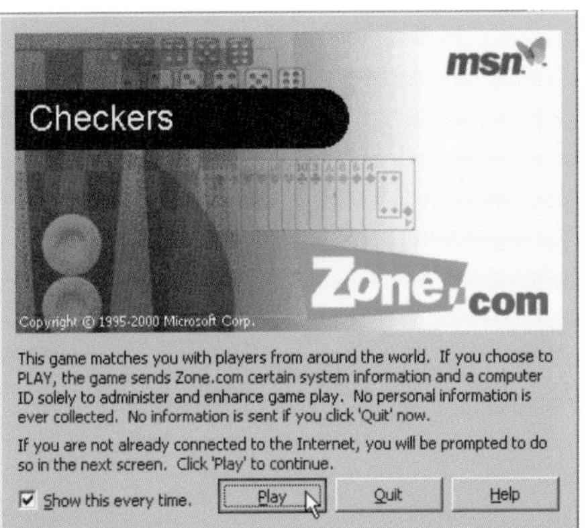

3 CONNECT TO GAMES SERVER

• A message tells you that an attempt is being made to connect you to the games server, which is at **Zone.com**.

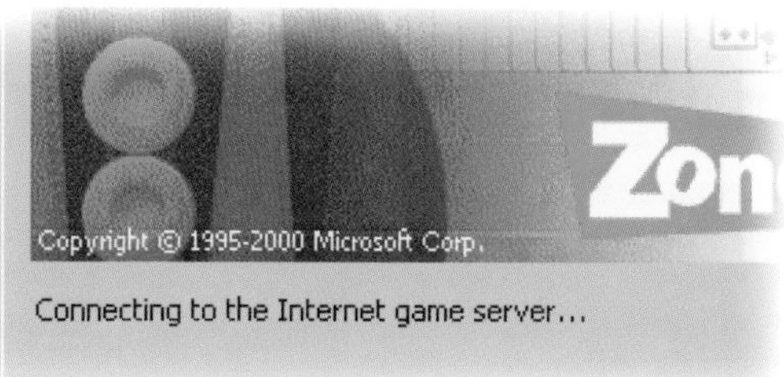

4 STARTING THE GAME

• Now you are launched straight into the fray, pitting your wits against an opponent who could be thousands of miles away.

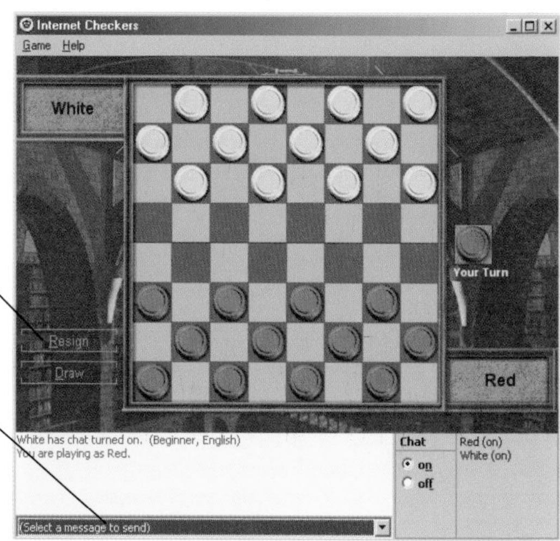

If you decide after a while that you just cannot win, you could always tactfully resign

*If you have the **Chat** button turned on, you can talk to your opponent by selecting a remark from the **Select a message to send** drop-down menu*

5 EXCHANGING MESSAGES

• Don't worry if you are playing someone whose language you do not understand, the message that you send from your computer will be translated at their end into their language and vice versa.

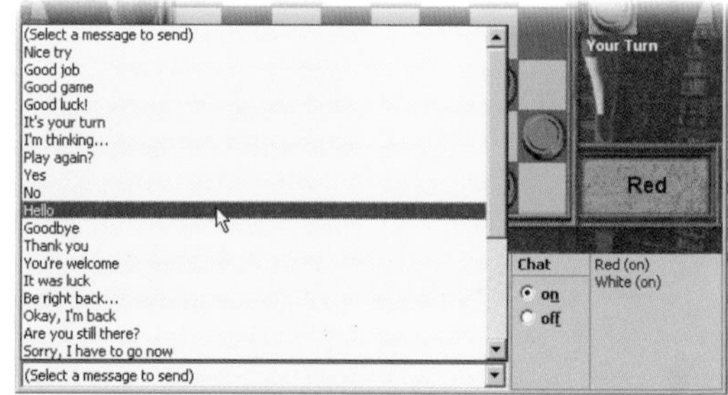

6 PLAYING ANOTHER GAME

- If you lose your game dismally, as we did here, either of the players can suggest another game, or the program offers you an opportunity to play another game against a new opponent.

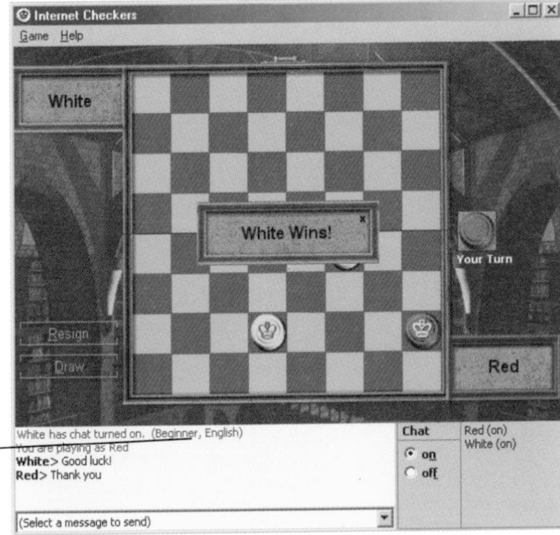

The language spoken by your opponent is given here

3D PINBALL SPACE CADET

- If you prefer a more fast-paced and immediate style of gaming, **3D Pinball Space Cadet** is worth trying – it's an exciting electronic version of a classic arcade pinball machine.
- The menu bar contains options to customize the game, and you can even listen to music or sound effects while you play.

GAMING ZONE

Microsoft's Gaming Zone, at **http://zone.msn.com**, has a **Game Index** link that lists all the games currently being played; one visit showed 110 games. Click on a game to see a list of games rooms and the total numbers playing.

GLOSSARY

APPLICATION
Another term for a piece of software, usually a program.

CD-ROM
Compact Disk – Read Only Memory. A disk containing data such as games and programs. Data can only be read from the disk, not written to it.

COMPRESSION
The act of reducing the size of a file by using software to compact or compress it.

DESKTOP
This screen, which appears once Windows Me has started up, displays the taskbar and, among other items, contains icons for My Documents and the Recycle Bin.

DELETE
To remove a document from its current location and place it in the Recycle Bin, from where it can be permanently deleted.

DOCUMENT
A document containing user data, such as text written in a word-processing program.

DOWNLOAD
Transferring data from one computer to another, usually over the internet.

EMAIL
A system for sending messages between computers that are linked electronically over a network.

FILE
A discrete collection of data stored on your computer.

FOLDER
A location for storing individual documents and other folders.

HARD DRIVE
The physical device on your computer where programs and files are stored.

ICON
A graphic symbol, attached to a file that indicates its type or the program it was created in.

INTERNET
The network of interconnected computers that communicate with one another.

INTERNET SERVICE PROVIDER
A business that provides a gateway to the internet.

MEDIA PLAYER
A program for playing and organizing multimedia on your computer and on the internet.

MODEM
A device used to connect a computer to the internet via a telephone line.

MOVIE MAKER
A part of Windows Me that turns your computer into an audio and video editing center.

MY COMPUTER
The entry point to your computer. Programs, files, and access to the disk drives are located here.

MY DOCUMENTS
A folder placed within Windows Me for use as a location to store your documents.

NETWORK
A collection of computers that are linked together.

PROGRAM
A software package that allows you to perform a specific task on your computer (also known as an application).

RECYCLE BIN
The location on your desktop where deleted files are stored. Files remain here until the Recycle Bin is emptied.

START MENU
Appears once the Start button has been clicked. Applications and documents can be accessed from here.

SOFTWARE
A computer needs software to function. Software ranges from simple utilities to immense computer games.

TASKBAR
The gray panel at the bottom of the desktop screen that contains the Start button, along with quick-access buttons to open programs and windows.

WINDOW
A panel displaying the contents of a folder or disk drive.

WINDOWS EXPLORER
A program for viewing and managing the contents of your computer.

WORLD WIDE WEB
The term used to refer to all the websites on the internet that are linked together to form a global web of information.

INDEX

ACKNOWLEDGMENTS

PUBLISHER'S ACKNOWLEDGMENTS
Dorling Kindersley would like to thank the following:
Paul Mattock of APM, Brighton, for commissioned photography.
www.tucows.com, www.google.com, www.zone.com
Microsoft Corporation for permission to reproduce screens
from within Microsoft® Windows® Me.

Screen shots of Microsoft® Windows® Me, Microsoft® Notepad, Microsoft® Paint, Imaging for Windows®, Microsoft® Wordpad, Microsoft® Windows® Explorer, Microsoft® Outlook Express, Microsoft® Internet Explorer, and Microsoft® Windows® Media Player used by permission from Microsoft Corporation.